ENDORSEMENTS FOR
UNMAPPED POTENTIAL

"Educators have an undeniable impact, which is only limited by their own beliefs and expectations. After all, beliefs inform actions, and actions create outcomes. In *Unmapped Potential*, Julie and Missy focus on changing limiting beliefs into empowering expectations. This is the fertile soil where the seeds of lasting change can grow."

—Jon Gordon, bestselling author of
The Energy Bus and *The Carpenter*

"This is an intriguing read for all educators! Driven by a call to action and motivated by personal experiences and heartfelt stories, Julie and Missy offer readers an optimistic perspective on education and how to best support the students we serve. The authors challenge each of us to create change, and they provide a valuable map for educators to forge their own inspiring journeys."

—Dr. Russell J. Quaglia, executive director, Quaglia Institute for
School Voice and Aspirations, author of *Student Voice, Parent
Voice, Teacher Voice,* and *Principal Voice*

"Through *Unmapped Potential: An Educator's Guide to Lasting Change*, you will explore your mental map, reflect on your beliefs, learn from mistakes, and make appropriate changes. Life is full of vicissitudes, so you should have a growth mindset instead of one that is fixed. The lessons learned from reading this insightful book will get you more comfortable with making the necessary revisions to enjoy your work and your life."

—Jerry Blumengarten (aka Cybraryman), keynote speaker and
author of *Connecting Your Students with the World*

"These educators understand that to address change effectively, a leader first must be reflective about his/her own practice. This book supports purposeful action rather than ineffective reaction to challenges. I have had the privilege of working with both of these outstanding leaders. Their actions are in line with their words. This book is a must-read for teachers and administrators!"

—Joyce Haines, Ph.D., M.Ed. program coordinator in educational leadership and policy studies at the University of South Florida

"In a world obsessed with the hopelessness and bureaucracy in education, this book leads the movement to shift the focus to the power every educational leader has on making a positive impact on their school and their students. Julie and Missy challenge educators to develop their mental maps—and the maps of others—to better navigate the changing educational topography."

—Jessica Solano, Florida Teacher of the Year 2017

"Super refreshing! This book captures the serious reality of an educator's life while weaving in humor and stories. An absolutely clear roadmap for you to achieve the potential you have in the treasure of who you are!"

—LaVonna Roth, international speaker, creator and founder of Ignite Your S.H.I.N.E.®

UNMAPPED Potential

AN EDUCATOR'S GUIDE TO LASTING CHANGE

Julie Hasson and Missy Lennard

Unmapped Potential

This book is available at special discounts when purchased in quantity for use as premiums, promotions, fundraisers, or for educational use. For inquiries and details, contact the publisher at shelley@daveburgessconsulting.com.

Published by Dave Burgess Consulting, Inc.
San Diego, CA
http://daveburgessconsulting.com

Cover Design by Genesis Kohler
Editing and Interior Design by My Writers' Connection

Library of Congress Control Number: 2017940166
Paperback ISBN: 978-1-946444-17-2
eBook ISBN: 978-1-946444-18-9

First Printing: May 2017

Dedication

THIS BOOK IS DEDICATED TO ALL
OF THE EDUCATORS WHO HELPED
THESE TWO SMALL-TOWN GIRLS
BELIEVE WE COULD LEAD SCHOOLS,
WRITE A BOOK, AND MAYBE EVEN
CHANGE SOME THINGS.

Contents

INTRODUCTION ix

CHAPTER 1
YOUR MAP MATTERS
3

CHAPTER 2
A CHANGE-SAVVY MAP
19

CHAPTER 3
CHOICE OR CHANCE
33

CHAPTER 4
MAPPING CHALLENGES AS OPPORTUNITIES
43

CHAPTER 5
YOUR MAP IMPACTS OTHERS
55

CHAPTER 6
PROSPECTING FOR POTENTIAL
67

CHAPTER 7
MOTIVATION ON THE MAP
79

CHAPTER 8
COLLABORATION IS THE KEY
89

CHAPTER 9
TRAVELING WITHIN THE SYSTEM
101

CHAPTER 10
YOU NEVER REALLY GET THERE
113

ACKNOWLEDGMENTS 117

RESOURCES 119

DISCOVER *UNMAPPED POTENTIAL* AT YOUR SCHOOL 121

MORE FROM DAVE BURGESS CONSULTING, INC. 122

ABOUT THE AUTHORS 131

Introduction

THE TWO OF US HAD DREAMED OF BEING SCHOOL PRINCIPALS, WITH VISIONS OF IMPROVING THE LIVES OF THE STUDENTS AND FAMILIES WE SERVED. But in the fall of 2012, we had to admit that things weren't going the way we had envisioned. We were two principals, each responsible for a diverse elementary school in one of the nation's largest school districts, constantly needing to accomplish more with fewer resources. We both became overwhelmed, overextended, and downright exhausted in our work. We propped ourselves up with caffeine and chocolate, but the fix was short-lived. Both of our schools were facing big challenges—rapidly growing student populations and changing demographics—yet we kept relying on the same old strategies. Clearly, we needed to serve our students differently. But we couldn't inspire needed change without becoming more effective and more inspiring. Our schools weren't going to change unless *we* did.

We met as members of a doctoral cohort in 2007, and we quickly connected through an affinity for iced tea, an unwavering devotion to James Taylor, and a common philosophy of education. We both believe that being mindful and intentional is foundational in teaching and leading, and we reject reactionary changes in favor of purposeful choices. We also believe in empowering students and teachers, giving them choice and voice. So, when we had the opportunity to open a new school in 2009 (Missy as principal and Julie as assistant principal), we jumped at the chance. We cherished our time working together, but by the fall of 2012, we had become fellow principals leading neighboring schools. As we supported each other in reflecting on our work and striving to grow, we realized that we were braver and wiser together than on our own; so we joined forces once again and embarked on a journey to improve ourselves *and* our schools. This book is the result of our continued partnership.

Whatever your role in education, you can probably relate to our struggles. When challenges come in rapid succession, it is tempting to react quickly rather than purposefully. But being in a continual state of reacting is not good for you or your students. Maybe you are feeling worn out, frustrated, or plagued by the nagging feeling you could be doing better. Maybe you are struggling to reach one student or to juggle one hundred. Maybe you begin each year with the best of intentions only to fizzle out by February. You are not alone.

We can't give you a prescription for eliminating all of your stress and struggles. (And, frankly, you should be wary of anyone who claims they can!) However, we can share the successful practices we observed in schools, found in a thorough review of research, and tried ourselves. We'll walk alongside you as you embark on your own journey of improvement. We'll encourage you, and even push you a bit to *apply* what you discover. Because knowing what to do isn't enough. Transformation happens when information meets application.

Unmapped Potential is a *self*-help book. We will give you tons of suggestions, and we're excited to support and encourage you; but in the end, you have to commit to doing the work to help yourself.

The first step in this journey is to examine your thoughts and beliefs—or your *mental map*, as we like to call it. During the course of your life, you have created a map full of assumptions, beliefs, and expectations. Your map shapes your thoughts. Your thoughts influence your actions. And the actions you take determine your outcomes. Thus, lasting change starts when you are brave enough to identify and modify the beliefs that are creating barriers on your map and holding you back from reaching your potential.

Once we took out our own mental maps, unfolded them, and *really* looked at them, we could see the limits we were placing on our students *and* ourselves. Up to that point, we had been unaware of the subtle (and not-so-subtle) messages we were sending to our students and colleagues every day. Through our words, actions, and choices, we were letting others know what we believed about their ability and potential, and sometimes those messages had a negative impact.

We were principals tasked with helping students and teachers grow, but we were actually impeding growth without knowing it. The tools we share in this book, combined with time and effort, helped us break through those limiting barriers. When that happened, we saw an upsurge in student achievement and accomplishment of "stretch goals." In the process, however, we messed up more times than we can count, but we learned from our mistakes—even more than we learned from our successes. Beyond those personal lessons, perhaps we have learned the most from the hundreds of educators all across the country who have connected with us during the writing of this book. When we shared our journey (missteps and all) at conferences and meetings, our colleagues shared their own struggles and strategies. Their contributions to this book are invaluable.

Unmapped Potential is part manifesto and part manual. Use it as a guide for identifying the changes you want to make and creating an action plan to see those changes through. Use the Map-Changing Questions at the end of each chapter to reflect on your own beliefs, and refer back to the Map-Changing Actions as often as needed. You might be tempted to skip these exercises, but we encourage you to resist that urge. Practice and reflection are essential parts of this journey. The illustrations at the beginning of each chapter (beautifully drawn by one of our favorite students) give an overview of the main concept of the chapter. Use them to think about what is on your own map related to the concepts. What you learn about yourself along the way will help you create a bold vision for the kind of educator you want to become and then chart a course to make that vision a reality.

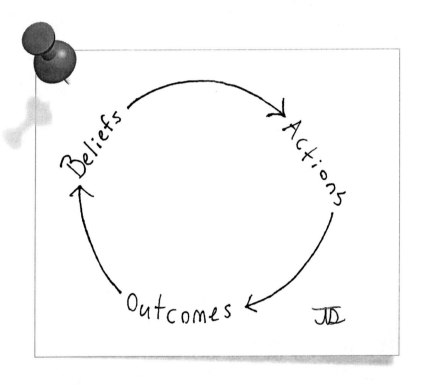

1
Your Map Matters

OUR FRIEND, JOE, TEACHES SOCIAL STUDIES AND IS AN AVID MAP COLLECTOR. In this era of high-tech navigation systems, kids are fascinated with maps. (They're so retro!) Joe keeps much of his collection in his classroom where students can do research or just explore. If you ask his students why these maps are still useful, they will enthusiastically argue the benefits of a good, old-fashioned map:

- Maps give you the big picture.
- Maps let you easily see the whole world all at once.
- Maps show how things are connected.
- Different maps show different things, from topography to politics.
- Maps show how borders have been transformed or names of places have been changed.

While visiting with Joe, it occurred to us that we are all guided by our own maps as we navigate the world. All our beliefs about ourselves and others, as well as the world and how it works, are represented in the maps we have created in our minds—our *mental maps*. Because our maps can empower or limit us, the place to start in the journey toward personal or professional improvement is to take out our maps, unfold and examine them.

As we travel across the country, talking with and learning from educators, we hear the same sentiment over and over: "Things have to change. Something's got to give." Educators tell us that the demands of their roles continue to increase while their resources shrink. Students come into their classrooms and schools with great needs, and working to meet those needs often stretches these educators to the breaking point. As teachers and leaders, we must reexamine our practices. Indeed, something needs to change. But big, bold change can be scary, and educators may feel paralyzed under the sheer magnitude of it. The truth is that the odds are against real, lasting change. We know this simply by looking at what happens every January. People begin the year with big plans for total-life overhauls. But within the first month, ninety-five percent of all resolutions and change initiatives are abandoned.

Maybe you feel comprehensive change is unobtainable. Maybe just thinking about big changes makes you want to hide out with Netflix and ice cream. So don't start big; start small. Admiral Charles McRaven once said, "If you want to change the world, start by making your bed." In other words, small, deliberate actions can lead to big transformations. Simple steps done with consistency and conviction can create a big impact. And making a small, positive change in one area will positively impact all other areas. These small changes create momentum. The starting place is each one of us simply examining and updating your mental map. Throughout this book, you will find ideas and strategies for discovering what is currently on your map as well as tips for revising your map.

Once you evaluate and update your mental map—breaking down those limiting barriers and creating empowering beliefs—the next step is to embrace those new beliefs and act on them. Several years ago, a determined kindergartener named Ben attended our school. Ben was like most other kindergarteners, except for one thing: He believed he could fly. He admitted he hadn't actually flown yet, but he was absolutely certain he *would* someday. He constantly drew pictures and told stories of his flying adventures. One day, as his class filed out to recess, a certain piece of playground equipment caught his eye. When his teacher finished tying another child's shoe, she looked up to see Ben on top of the monkey bars. Before she could stop him, he jumped! Fearing he'd hurt himself, she ran toward him but discovered he wasn't hurt at all. In fact, she could hear Ben yelling, "Did you see that? I did it! I flew!"

We are not advocating jumping off the monkey bars, but we *are* suggesting belief plus action helps you realize your goals. Ben's belief he could fly influenced his decision to jump. Belief came first; action followed. Don't miss the true power of beliefs; they influence every action you choose to take—or choose not to take. And those actions (or inactions) create outcomes.

EVERY OUTCOME BEGINS
WITH A SINGLE THOUGHT.

The reality is that every outcome begins with a single thought. If a thought sticks around long enough, it becomes a pattern and, eventually, turns into a belief. That belief either turns into an action or leads to inaction. Repeated behaviors (action *or* inaction) become habits, and habits either draw things into your life or keep them out. Think about it: Good health stems from healthy eating and exercise habits. Good relationships stem from small, positive interactions and gestures over time. Consistent actions shape your habits, and your habits shape your life. How is your current map impacting your actions and outcomes?

Unfortunately, most people move through life unaware of the mental map that guides their thoughts, choices, and, thus, their outcomes. Few people deliberately consider the contents of their mental maps.

THE CARTOGRAPHER OF YOUR MENTAL MAP

Throughout your life, you have been acting as an unwitting cartographer, taking notes and marking landmarks based on what you have seen, experienced, expected, and assumed about how the world works. Let's take a look at some of the things that have shaped the topography of your mental map. We'll start with an overview here and then explore these ideas together in more detail in the following chapters.

BOUNDARIES (AKA LIMITING BELIEFS)

Limiting beliefs mark the borders of your potential—for yourself, your career, your school, and your students. You can only achieve that which you believe you are capable and worthy. You can focus on changing behavior or environment, but without attending to your beliefs, those changes will be short term. Like a sturdy rubber band, you may be able to stretch your limits temporarily, but you will always snap back to where you ultimately *believe* you belong. The only way to move past a limiting belief is to break it. Just like breaking a rubber band, breaking a limiting belief is uncomfortable; but the freedom of moving beyond that limiting belief is worth the discomfort.

ROUGH REPRESENTATIONS

Geographical maps never fully depict the actual territory. Cartographers mark what they see—but if you travel the same road, you may see something the mapmaker missed. Each person's mental map is simply a representation based on that individual's unique beliefs and perceptions. Therefore, everyone's map is slightly (and sometimes not-so-slightly) skewed by personal experiences and perspective. Imagine how this impacts the classroom. The teacher's map is different from each student's individual map—and every person in the classroom believes his or her map is the correct one. What if the teacher's map defines *smart* as doing well on assignments and performing well on tests, but one of her students defines it as the ability to navigate the social norms of the neighborhood and survive? Since the teacher and student both believe their map is the correct one, they can't understand the choices and actions of the other.

You must accept two important statements in order to begin the deep dive into your reality-shaping beliefs: (1) Your map is not *the* territory, and (2) your map is different from everyone else's map. All maps are a skewed picture of reality. Likewise, all maps become outdated over time, which brings us to the next point.

EXAMINING YOUR MAP

Maybe some of your beliefs aren't serving you well. If so, we have good news. As explorers Ferdinand Magellan and Vasco da Gama did when they discovered something new about a location, you can update your mental map whenever you acquire new information.

We don't want to give you the wrong impression; changing your map is not easy. The longer you carry your map around, the harder it will be to change. When you arrived on this planet as a bouncing, beautiful bundle of joy, you were fully present. You were content just to experience and explore, driven only by your physical needs. Before long, you began to receive messages about what is right and wrong, scary and safe, valuable and worthless from those older than you. From those early judgments, you formed beliefs, which carved pathways in the subconscious part of your brain. These pathways may have remained largely unexplored and unquestioned throughout your life. Today, while the conscious part of your brain takes attendance, locates lesson plans, and ponders what's for lunch, the beliefs in the caverns of your subconscious mind quietly influence your thoughts and actions.

EFFICIENCY VS. ACCURACY

From birth, you experience the world through sight, smell, touch, sound, and taste. With so much information to process, your brain seeks ways to operate more efficiently. Without even having to think about it, you (and all other humans!) do three things that keep you from shutting down due to information overload. First, you *generalize*. You look for similarities between your current experiences and your previous experiences. Second, you *delete*. You release or ignore information inconsistent with your predetermined notions. Third, you *distort*. You change aspects of an experience to fit the existing patterns in your mind. Once your brain forms a pattern, your subconscious mind goes to great lengths to maintain that pattern. For example, have you ever talked to two people who have completely different recollections of the same event and wondered how they could have witnessed things so differently? Their memories are different because each viewed the event through their individual maps. Based on their previous experiences, they generalized, deleted, and distorted to create a reality based on their existing beliefs. They each interpreted the event in a way that made sense to them.

> CULTIVATING AWARENESS IS LIKE GETTING A SHOT. IT IS NECESSARY FOR YOUR WELL-BEING, AND IT HURTS MUCH MORE WHEN YOU TENSE UP AND RESIST IT.

These automated thoughts and behaviors may help you survive, but they don't allow you to *thrive*. Thriving requires bringing your beliefs into consciousness, something that may be challenging and uncomfortable. Cultivating awareness is like getting a shot. It is necessary for your well-being, and it hurts much more when you tense up and resist it.

Even though the two of us lead seminars on how to discover and expand possibilities, exploring our own thought patterns and belief systems can still feel unsettling or scary at times. We have avoided self-discovery by living in the past ("Those were the good old days!") or living in the future ("Things will be better when …"). We avoided uncomfortable self-reflection by numbing ourselves, finding distractions, and constantly staying busy. (Trust us—we can surf the Internet and rearrange our paperclip collections like pros!)

Unfortunately, it is not possible to numb selective aspects of life. When you numb fear, anger, and insecurity, you also numb joy, love, and creativity. We were missing the wise and innovative parts of ourselves by avoiding the seemingly difficult things. You, too, are your own best expert, but you may be unable to hear your intuitive and creative thoughts through the white noise of distractions. When you decide to embrace the challenge of attending to your inner wisdom, your internal compass will point you in the right direction, and you will begin to uncover the true potential hidden by your existing map. How might you be resisting the examination of your map?

UNDERSTANDING THE LEGEND

Your map holds your expectations and beliefs and ultimately colors the world in which you live. Why does this matter to your work in education? First, your beliefs impact your own success and well-being which, in turn, impacts the way you teach and lead. Second, the messages you send about your expectations impact those you teach and lead. Students and colleagues are constantly picking up cues about your beliefs and expectations.

One of our principal friends, Kim, works with a dynamic team of first grade teachers who perform a character-education play every year. During a calendaring meeting one September, Kim asked for the date of the play, and the team leader informed her that they had decided to skip the play this year. Although Kim was disappointed, she tried not to show it, knowing they had many new things to tackle during the school year. To Kim's surprise, the team leader stopped by her office the next day to give her the date they had chosen for the play. When Kim asked why they had changed their minds, the team leader responded they had reconsidered when they noticed Kim's disappointment. Even though Kim hadn't said anything at the meeting, everyone in the room saw the disappointment on Kim's face. She had communicated a powerful message without saying a word.

Like Kim, you may not be aware that you communicate your beliefs in subtle and not-so-subtle ways—all day, every day. In fact, even when you are silent, you are communicating.

REDRAWING THE MAP

As an educator, you are constantly communicating. However, your most important communication is not what you share with others; it is the continual chatter of the voice inside your head. Self-talk can be empowering or limiting, and you must bring it into consciousness in order to change its patterns. For example, when adversity or unwelcome events happen, pay attention to your thoughts. Do you use words like *always* or *never*? These words are clues your thinking is exacerbating a difficult situation and preventing you from effective problem-solving. Using limiting self-talk negatively impacts your outcomes as well as your learning and growth.

In order to change and grow, you must reflect back on your experiences. The very best time to examine thought patterns and beliefs may be *during* a difficult situation. While in the throes of adversity, pay attention to what you are thinking. Are your thoughts helping or harming you? Your emotions are always a big clue. Immediately examine your thoughts when you feel agitated, frustrated, angry, or worried. Ask yourself if you want these particular thoughts to influence your actions. Are these the thoughts you would want to create your outcomes? Contrast those thoughts with your thoughts when you are feeling positive emotions, like serenity, gratitude or joy. Would these thoughts create better outcomes? Your emotions are typically aroused more by your thoughts about a situation than the actual situation itself.

The following story about Mark, a fifth-grade student, demonstrates the power of thoughts to arouse emotions. Mark noticed one day that his favorite eraser was missing. He was certain another student had taken it and became very angry at the thought of a classmate intentionally disrespecting him by taking something that belonged to him. The teacher offered him a new eraser, but that didn't' make him feel better. The situation itself (a missing eraser) was not the source of his anger. Instead, his anger was rooted in his thoughts and assumptions about the situation. When a friend found the eraser on the floor near Mark's desk, the teacher took the opportunity to talk with Mark about the connection between thoughts and emotions.

You may not be able to relate to or understand Mark's anger over a missing eraser. But in that moment, Mark believed he was perfectly justified in his feelings and actions. You probably recall a time when your thoughts and assumptions led to negative emotions and regrets. Your personal beliefs and the way you express them may seem seriously twisted to others at times. However, your beliefs and behaviors always make sense to *you* because they are based on your unique map. If you could rewind your life and watch it from the beginning, you would see when and why you formed certain patterns and beliefs.

Our kindergarten teacher friend, Kay, realized that whenever she sketched something while teaching, she apologized to her students, saying, "I can't draw." When one of her students asked her why she always said that, Kay remembered a very critical art teacher she had as a young child. On more than one occasion, the teacher had harshly evaluated and crumpled up her work. That criticism had carved a pathway in Kay's psyche, a loop labeled "I can't draw." For years, she had retraced that loop anytime she attempted to sketch an idea. Her student's question made Kay consider *why* she had that limiting belief. Rather than accepting her old teacher's limitation, Kay took an art class and discovered she loved to draw. (She broke that confining rubber band!) In fact, with practice, she became quite the artist.

Becoming aware of her "I can't draw" reflex was the first step toward breaking the limiting belief. With that self-awareness came the realization that Kay had the ability to replace those thoughts with empowering ones. One art class at a time, she redrew her mental map; and by doing so, she showed her students the difference between current reality and her potential. She became a powerful model for her students and colleagues.

Like Kay, most people tend to believe everything they say to themselves—without question. This is especially unfortunate, since thoughts and self-talk are not just reactions to events; they can actually *change* outcomes. You may have heard of the connection between beliefs and outcomes referred to as a self-fulfilling prophecy. In other words, what you expect to happen actually happens, just as you expected. Even if your expectations are built on completely false assumptions, you will likely act in ways that work to make those false beliefs come true. For example, if you believe your new boss does not like you, you may be anxious or negative at work. Your anxiety and negativity may lead to mistakes and, eventually, tough feedback from your boss. Your belief is then affirmed—your boss clearly doesn't like you! Or maybe you fear being late to work. In your rushing around, you spill your coffee, have to change your clothes, and clean up a mess. Sure enough, you are late—just as you expected.

Thankfully, it is just as easy to expect a positive outcome as it is to expect a negative one. It takes just as much energy to believe things will be totally awesome instead of totally awful, so choose awesome! If you convince yourself something is true, you will find plenty of evidence to support it. What limiting beliefs are you unintentionally confirming?

WHAT'S YOUR DESTINATION?

You probably find it easy to believe in things you have seen or experienced, but believing in the unseen is a challenge. Believing in things you have not yet experienced is called having vision. Creating a powerful vision requires clarity about the outcomes you desire plus enough imagination to paint a mental picture of those realized outcomes. Having a vision is like putting a destination on your map. When you know where you are and know where you are going, you can plan a route to get there. Big, transformational change is dependent on vision. So develop your vision, nurture it, and hold unwavering belief in it. The possibilities are so much bigger and wider than your experiences to this point. Don't let your past limit your map.

Honestly looking at your map and examining what you really believe is essential because your beliefs can lead you to behave in ways that produce unintended, negative consequences for yourself, your colleagues, and your school. How do you know when you are harboring beliefs and expectations out of alignment with what you truly want? As we said earlier, your emotions provide clues. Another way to identify limiting beliefs is to examine any area in which you consistently fall short of your goals. When you eat the brownies (all six of them) despite a goal for improved health, you have found an area for examination. When you set a school-wide goal to improve student behavior, but out-of-school suspension rates increase, you need to determine why. Observable evidence on the outside indicates what is going on inside. The beliefs we have about ourselves, other people, and the world influence our actions. If we change our beliefs, we change our actions. New actions lead to different outcomes, and different outcomes confirm the new beliefs. If you really want to change the outcomes you are experiencing, first change your patterned thoughts and beliefs.

Hanging on to our existing beliefs, even when they don't serve us well, is human nature. After all, we have been seeing things for years not as they are, but as we *believe* they are. So we make choices to reinforce our sense of security and maintain the status quo. We play it safe and maintain familiar habits, even when we say we want different results. Most of us never stop to question the accuracy of our beliefs. We go about our days looking through the lens of the beliefs and expectations we have formed about ourselves, about others, and about the world. We automatically make things fit into our preconceived patterns. But if we will take the time and develop the tools, we can change the mental map reflecting our beliefs. We can change limiting beliefs into empowering beliefs. And by doing so, we can create a map to help us realize a powerful vision for ourselves, our students, our schools, and ultimately, our world.

Map-Changing Actions

Construct a simple timeline of significant moments or major events in your life. Consider how these events shaped your map. Have your perceptions of these events contributed to limiting or empowering beliefs? The emotions you feel when you remember these events and the outcomes you continue to experience will give you clues. Think about whether the beliefs you continue to carry are leading to the outcomes you desire. Identify one or two beliefs or patterns you would like to change.

Map-Changing Questions

1. Identify an area where your results are consistently different from the goals you set.

2. What are your past experiences related to this?

3. What are the stories you tell yourself related to success in this area?

4. What would you need to do differently to experience different results?

5. Why aren't you consistently doing that?

SHARE YOUR JOURNEY
WITH OTHER MAP
CHANGERS USING THE
#UNMAPPEDED HASHTAG.

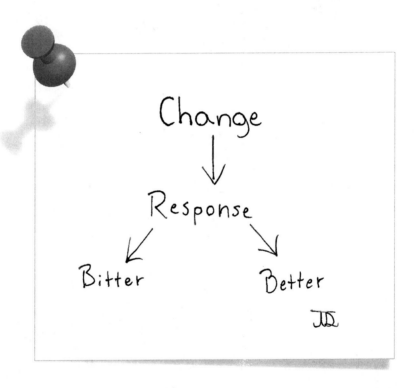

A Change-Savvy Map

WE LIVE IN FLORIDA WHERE IT IS HOT ABOUT 360 DAYS OF THE YEAR. To beat the heat and reward students for making good choices in the lunchroom, our teachers occasionally give students ice pops. For one of Mary's four-year-old students, unfortunately, this reward turned into heartbreak. Mary was shocked to discover this little guy had carried his ice pop with him from the lunchroom and tucked it "safely" inside his desk. At the end of the day when he pulled it out, there was nothing but orange liquid sloshing around inside the plastic packet. Inconsolable, he cried, "I was saving it for later!" Mary captured the teachable moment to explain states of matter, and her student learned a hard lesson: Change is inevitable.

No matter how old you are, change is a certainty in this uncertain world. Any change has the potential to make you bitter or better; the difference is in how you *respond* to that change. Change *will* elicit a response, and your map plays a crucial role in the quality of that response. Author and activist Howard Zinn said, "You can't be neutral on a moving train." As you travel through life, the landscape is continually changing. You are always moving forward or backward; there is no standing still. As an educator, your work is ever changing—new students, new schedules, new curriculum, new policies, and countless other new elements. Changes can occur simultaneously and rapidly. You may not be able to control all of them and the challenges they bring. But you can always control your response to change.

NAVIGATING CHANGE

What kind of mental map is most effective for navigating change? One that is simultaneously realistic and optimistic, focused and flexible. Any change is challenging because it requires us to leave our comfort zones, those fear-based states designed to keep us safely locked inside our current realities. That's why changing roles, grade levels or subject areas is frightening to many educators. You may be better suited or have greater impact in a new role, but the resistance to making such a change is strong. Comfort zones are based on our current maps, which may be full of limiting beliefs. Replacing those limiting beliefs with empowering ones allows us to leave our comfort zones and move into our potential zones.

Your *potential zone* is a proactive state where you actively change your map and create your reality. This is the arena of awesomeness—where the "magic" happens. But to get to this zone, you will have to challenge your resistance to change and your fear of the unknown. You will also have to resist the bystanders who become fearful and uncomfortable simply watching you embrace change in order to break out of a rut. How willing are you to abandon what is comfortable?

DIP AHEAD!

Along with discomfort, change may also trip up your journey with the *implementation dip*, the lag in performance you're likely to experience when you leave behind old ways in favor of new strategies. Initially, you are sure to perform worse—at least for a little while. This implementation dip is the reason many people give up early and decide too soon that new strategies are no good. For example, as principals, we have both taken on the challenge of overhauling dismissal procedures at schools for the sake of safety and efficiency. When we first changed the procedures, dismissing students took a lot longer than it had previously. Everyone involved (from car riders to bus drivers) was learning the new system, and, at first, our staff members and students' parents begged us to go back to the old system. But after a few weeks of practice, dismissal became super safe and speedy. We survived the inevitable dip in performance and reached our intended destination.

Chances are, you have a patterned, routine way of responding to change and unexpected challenges. Your response largely determines how smoothly and quickly you will navigate the new landscape. Simply put, your way of responding likely falls toward either the optimistic or the pessimistic side of a continuum. Optimists respond with hope and possibility. When adversity surfaces, optimists view it as temporary and context specific—meaning things will improve when the situation changes. In other words, optimists are able to envision a positive outcome and limit the negative impact of adversity. For example, when a new student with challenging behaviors enrolled in our friend Beth's third-grade class, her comments revealed her optimistic outlook. She talked about how she could help the student acclimate to her expectations, but she also asserted that she would teach him with the same love and respect given other students even if his behavior didn't significantly change. And she optimistically added, "He will be headed for fourth grade come summer."

Pessimistic thinking, on the other hand, is grounded in permanence and pervasiveness. Pessimists tend to catastrophize unwanted circumstances. They view challenges as never ending, and the negative energy from one event spills over into all areas of their lives. For example, if Beth were a pessimist, she might have viewed the new student as evidence kids were becoming less respectful, and her job would inevitably become harder as a result. She'd be convinced that the stress from her job would inevitably impact her health and her relationships negatively. In fact, a pessimistic Beth might be searching for a new job right now!

Viewing adversity as permanent and pervasive only leads to despair and helplessness. Pessimistic people can easily find themselves caught in a cycle of giving up. After experiencing several challenges or setbacks in a row, they feel discouraged and may feel as if it takes more effort to keep going. Then, because they feel weak, they begin to avoid difficult tasks. Avoidance leads to negative consequences and more adversity, the challenge-avoidance cycle perpetuates, and they get stuck.

GET A BETTER VIEW

The best way to get a better view is to clean your windshield. In other words, the filter of your own perspective may be making the landscape itself appear more dismal. For example, Kyle, a physical education teacher, was part of a committee tasked with organizing a school health fair. Unfortunately, the results were not what Kyle had hoped for; the health fair seemed chaotic and did not have a great turnout. Kyle could have listened to negative self-talk: *I never work well with others. I'm just not a leader. This health fair was a really bad idea.* If he had allowed himself to dwell on the event with a sense of pessimism, those thoughts would have continued, working to convince him that the poor outcome of the event was due to a personal characteristic that was unlikely to change. Instead, Kyle changed his self-talk: "Our group did not communicate well, and we needed more time. Now we know how to improve in order to have a more successful fair next year." His optimistic explanation focused on changeable factors within the situation. As a result, the future seems brighter, and he and his team will be ready to take on the next challenge instead of staying stuck in a hopeless place. You can do the same! Change your frame and change the situation.

Argue back against the self-talk that paints a pessimistic view of change or challenges. Objectively understanding and taking responsibility for your role in any outcome is essential to personal growth, but beating yourself up is never helpful. How often do you convince yourself that events are permanent and pervasive rather than temporary and context specific?

Arguing with yourself may seem silly—but it works. One strategy for taming negative self-talk is to name the voice inside your head. Our friend, Jill, calls hers "Ethel." When Ethel starts chattering, Jill thanks her for her concern and politely tells her to be quiet. You may think the negative voice in your head is your true inner voice of wisdom and intuition, but it's not. It's just Ethel.

The words you use to frame change or a challenging situation undoubtedly impact the outcome. For example, when a student is struggling in your class, you may frame the situation with the following words: *This student has no support at home; he will never do well in my class.* However, that leaves little room for productive problem-solving. On the other hand, words like *I will find ways to get support for this student so he can be successful* promote solutions. Think about your mental response to the following situations and consider whether your reaction tends to be limiting or empowering:

When preparing to talk to an overinvolved parent …

She is making me crazy; I will never live up to her unreasonable expectations. (Limiting)

I need to find ways to reassure her so we can agree on a reasonable plan. (Empowering)

When you get an email about a required professional development activity …

This is a waste of time; I never learn anything at these sessions. (Limiting)

I will look for at least one new idea for improving my practice. (Empowering)

When asked to assist a new teacher …

I don't have time to help someone else. I can barely keep up myself. (Limiting)

I could learn some new strategies from this young teacher, and I can reflect on my own practice while mentoring. (Empowering)

In each scenario, there is only one situation but two vastly different outcomes depending on what you tell yourself. The words you use to describe your reality define your reality.

CURVES AHEAD!

Mental flexibility, the ability to adjust your thinking in response to a changing environment, is the most useful tool in your toolbox for dealing with challenges and change. Being mentally flexible allows you to think about a problem in a new way, consider multiple perspectives, and choose the best response. When educators and students practice flexible thinking, they are better able to cope with changing demands and new contexts, both inside and outside the classroom. A flexible mind moves one from limited options to endless solutions.

One of our favorite illustrations of flexible thinking involved a mother with significant hearing loss who came into our school office to sign out her son for an appointment. The secretary tried to explain to the mother that it would take several minutes for her son to get to the office because he was outside beyond the athletic field. Unfortunately, because of her hearing loss, the mom couldn't understand. The secretary repeated the information, speaking louder, but it didn't help. A teacher tried to give the message in sign language, but his signs were rusty. Everyone was getting frustrated. Finally, the mail carrier came into the office and wrote the secretary's message on a piece of paper for the mom. Her flexible thinking provided the needed solution to the problem.

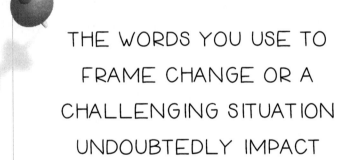

THE WORDS YOU USE TO FRAME CHANGE OR A CHALLENGING SITUATION UNDOUBTEDLY IMPACT THE OUTCOME.

Effective teachers use flexible thinking every day. They assist students who have not yet mastered the content and enrich those who mastered the content quickly by trying different approaches and strategies. After all, each student responds differently. What worked with last year's class may not work with this year's class. In fact, a lesson that worked well last period may not work next period. The most effective teachers are continually learning new things from their students and colleagues. And they are tweaking new approaches and strategies through practice. Effective teachers are irrefutably flexible.

How do you develop mental flexibility? Add some novelty to your day. Change your route or your routine. Learn something new—a new dance, language, or recipe. People often think growth happens after they do something, when they reflect on the experience; however, your brain is growing and changing *as* you learn something. Just think about the awareness and flexibility you could employ as your students teach you how to do the "running man" at recess. Scientists call this neuroplasticity, the endless potential of our brains to learn and grow. The more novelty you give your brain, the more pathways you create, and the more flexible you become. The brain will literally change itself with the right kinds of experiences. After all, you can't get someplace new with the same old thoughts and actions. Filling your days with what is predictable leaves little room for what else is possible.

FILLING YOUR DAYS WITH WHAT IS PREDICTABLE LEAVES LITTLE ROOM FOR WHAT ELSE IS POSSIBLE.

ALTERNATE ROUTES

In addition to mental flexibility, effectively navigating change also requires confidence. Confident learners are comfortable with complexity and are willing to experiment. They are not afraid of the unknown because they can recall and relate past successes to new experiences. Like we said at one of our former schools (whose mascot was a cowboy, by the way): *This is not our first rodeo.* In other words, we have successfully dealt with challenges in the past and have the ability to do it again. Confident learners embrace challenges and take the proverbial bull by the horns.

But what happens when change is needed yet ignored? Schools can be great at reproduction, producing the same outcomes over and over again, despite the need to do something different. If ignored for too long, the need for change at some point becomes obvious and urgent, and we panic. As a result, we may adopt changes not based on our specific needs or issues, or we may even embark on a rapid succession of change initiatives. Our friend, Lisa, is the new principal of a high-needs school with a history of low scores on annual achievement tests. As Lisa reviewed the initiatives that have been imposed on the school in the past two years, she counted more than twenty new programs. In this case, Lisa expressed a need to drop out of the race to the next new thing, find strategies to slow the adoption of potentially ineffective change, and focus on finding the right change.

When you recognize a need for change and want to change on purpose with purpose, you focus. You may see indicators in your classrooms or schools that you are not serving students well in some area. Successful change efforts depend on your ability to act when you identify a need. You must first create a compelling *why*—a good rationale for the change. Most schoolwide problems are not simple and easy to identify. Instead, they are impacted by numerous sources, requiring thoughtful analysis and continual adjustments. Our friend and reading coach, Emily, tried to create purposeful change at her school because the faculty was stuck in a rut and needed to revise their reading instruction. Instead of waiting for everyone to get on board, she started a *Coalition of the Willing* ("C.O.W."). As the C.O.W. made changes and began to see success, others began to join the movement until a new way of working with readers took hold school-wide. As Emily discovered, sometimes you just have to communicate a compelling purpose, take action, and let the forward momentum propel you.

One key to effective and lasting change in schools is to correctly identify the problem. Finding the right solution is impossible when focused on solving the wrong problem. Our friend, Brian, an assistant principal at an elementary school, found a glaring issue in the school's discipline data. Data broken down by student ethnicity and gender showed a disproportionate number of discipline incidences and consequences for certain groups of students. He immediately began to put extra support in place for these students—from mentoring to rewards—but saw little change. Finally, he asked another assistant principal, whose school was known for successfully changing discipline practices, what had made the difference. What he discovered was a cultural responsiveness training that the school had offered their teachers, which had led to significant improvement. Brian had never considered better equipping his teachers *in addition to* supporting improved behavior in his students. He realized the problem was more complex than he originally thought.

As Brian discovered, many good ideas for dealing with change stem from examining the practices of those who are succeeding where we are not. Sometimes, the best answers do not come from experts, researchers, or consultants; they come from our colleagues down the street. Implementers learn from other implementers who are just one or two steps ahead. Have you ever gone to a conference seeking an innovative way to address a problem and found that the best ideas came from attendees rather than experts? We've experienced this more times than we can count! Leverage connections with fellow practitioners and reap the benefits. Engage in conversations with colleagues who are also on the path to positive, purposeful change.

Consider one note of caution as you identify positive changes and work toward putting them into practice. Many of us spend so much time preparing to change that we never even get to the implementation part. Planning can be very seductive because there is no failure in planning. As a result, we can become stuck in the planning phase forever. We have a friend who is always preparing to start a weight loss program. He picks up the fitness class schedule, signs up for the nutrition classes, buys new workout clothes, and visits the self-help section at the bookstore. He is in an endless cycle of preparing but never taking action. Remember: The detail and prettiness of the plan has absolutely nothing to do with the outcome. Once you have a plan, be willing to get on with it. Don't get so involved in the "ready" and the "aim" that you never "fire."

While you may not be able to anticipate all the changes ahead, you can be certain change *is* coming. Although many of the changes and challenges you encounter are beyond your control, you can always decide how you will respond to them. You can frame them in hopeful ways and talk to yourself in empowering statements. Certain change is necessary and intentional and, with the right kind of thinking, you can get through the dip. When you remain flexible in your thinking, you are better able to generate plans and possible solutions. Embrace change when it's needed, and make that change with purpose. Tap into the expertise of colleagues and follow their patterns for success. Responding to change in ways that make you better, not bitter, is a powerful step in revising your map.

Map-Changing Actions

The best way to prepare for change and unexpected challenges is to practice flexible thinking. Rigid thinkers love rules and routines. While rules can certainly come in handy at times, fixating on them can make it hard to be flexible. Try changing the rules to your favorite board game. Making small changes to the rules can make games more fun and improve your ability to solve problems. Like rules, routines are a great source of comfort because they help us predict what comes next. Unfortunately, dependence on routines sometimes increases rigid thinking. In order to develop flexible thinking, make small tweaks to your routine instead of doing everything exactly the same way each day. Even small changes, like taking a different route or trying a new recipe, are enough to spark some flexibility. If you want to go bigger, try a new hobby, language, or musical instrument.

Map-Changing Questions

1. What are your patterned ways of responding to change?

2. What do you tend to say to yourself when unexpected challenges arise?

3. What strategies do you use to identify a problem, make a plan, and take action?

4. In what ways could you add some novelty and flexibility to your professional life?

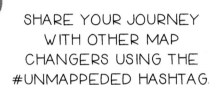

SHARE YOUR JOURNEY
WITH OTHER MAP
CHANGERS USING THE
#UNMAPPEDED HASHTAG.

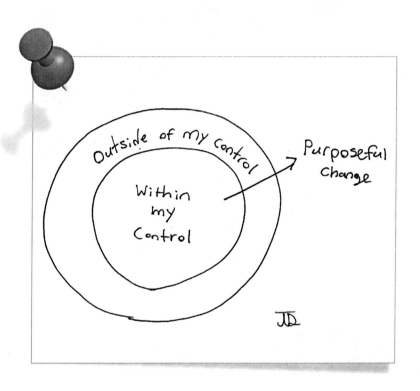

Choice or Chance

A S FLORIDIANS, WE HAVE SEEN OUR SHARE OF HURRICANES. Although we receive several days of warning when a hurricane is approaching, it is difficult to predict exactly where it will hit and how strong it will be. Even locations outside the center of the storm may experience significant damage due to tornadoes and flooding. Meteorologists here are fond of saying, "Prepare for the worst, but hope for the best." They urge us to take care of things we can control, such as securing lawn furniture and boarding up windows, and encourage us to remain cautiously optimistic about what we can't control: Mother Nature's impact. While this is good advice in hurricane weather, it also applies when other life storms arise. We need to focus on and apply our efforts to what we can control, and accept the things we can't control without wasting our time and energy on them.

WHO (OR WHAT) IS LEADING THE WAY?

How much power do you have over the circumstances of your life? Do you believe you can change things for the better, or do you believe your circumstances dictate your outcomes? Your answers influence your choices and results. The difference depends upon the locus of control you use. If you rely on an internal locus of control, you believe your own behavior determines your outcomes and, with effort, you can improve your situation. If you use an external locus of control, you attribute your outcomes to luck, fate, chance, or the power of others. Locus of control exists on a continuum. You are not fully on one side or the other of the continuum, but you likely have tendencies toward one side.

INTERNAL COMPASS

Let's illustrate this in a classroom setting. A teacher's lesson does not go well. If the teacher is using an internal locus of control, his thoughts might include: *I need to reteach some prerequisite skills. I need to explain these concepts in a different way. I need to plan more hands-on practice for these students.* By contrast, a teacher using an external locus of control might think: *The students are just not motivated. They never pay attention. They just don't care, and their parents don't care either.* Clearly, the teacher with an internal locus of control sees opportunities to positively impact the situation and feels empowered to change things for the better. The teacher with an external locus of control feels victimized by circumstances.

An external locus of control can easily lead to a phenomenon called *learned helplessness.* When we believe we cannot influence an outcome because our behaviors are unrelated to the outcome, we feel helpless.

When educators and students perceive they have no control, they give up easily and are not able to effectively problem solve. In fact, they are unlikely even to attempt a challenging task. We once worked with a teacher who had convinced himself he was helpless with technology and became unwilling to try new tech tools. He gladly let others do tech-related tasks for him, despite our encouragement. As a result of his expectations ("I can't be successful with technology so I won't even try."), he missed some great opportunities for growth.

EXTERNAL DRIVERS

On the contrary, positive expectations ("I *can* so I *will*.") are powerful predictors of success. Have you ever set the same goal multiple times yet never reached it? Would you be surprised to know the biggest obstacle to your success might the person looking back at you in the mirror? Your beliefs about yourself and your abilities largely determine whether or not you reach your goals. Remember your map—those core beliefs? In the case of unmet goals, your map is not getting you to your desired destination.

When it comes to success, two areas of belief matter:

- what you believe about your own ability to produce results; and

- what you believe happens as the result of your environment.

If you believe the world is biased, unresponsive, or out to get you, you will resist challenge. To be successful, you need positive outcome expectations and positive efficacy expectations. An *outcome expectation* is simply the belief a certain behavior will produce a certain outcome. An *efficacy expectation* is the belief you can effectively perform the behavior required to produce the outcome. We may believe an action will bring about a result, but if we doubt we can perform the action, we are sunk. Both beliefs are necessary. If a student believes knowing math facts leads to greater math proficiency, and she also believes she has the capacity to learn math facts, she will likely begin to study math facts and persist at the task. Likewise, if a teacher believes it is possible for all students to succeed, and he believes he has the skills to facilitate their success, he will rock his classroom.

SIGNS, LABELS, AND MILE MARKERS

As we have discussed, the brain loves patterns, and it automatically sorts everything into two main categories—*Me* and *Not Me*. Although this sounds simple, it has a huge impact on your success. For example, when you see a pair of running shoes, do you automatically assign those to *Me*—or *Not Me*? Perhaps you categorize objects related to good health as *Not Me* and then wonder why you can't adopt healthy habits. The truth is that you will never achieve goals you set if you unknowingly place items related to those goals in *Not Me*. You will only achieve what you believe you are capable and worthy of based on your map.

The relationship between beliefs and behavior is a bit like considering the chicken and the egg. Your self-perceptions are based on the actions you take (or don't take). Conversely, changing your behaviors can also help you see yourself differently. For example, you may not consider yourself a runner. "Runner" may be quickly assigned to the *Not Me* category. So how can you begin to see yourself as a runner? You run. As you continue running over a period of time, you will move "runner" from the *Not Me* to the *Me* category. Similarly, we have met many teachers for whom "principal" falls squarely into their *Not Me*. However, as they accept leadership tasks in their schools, they often begin to see themselves differently, and "principal" becomes a new possibility. What are you automatically placing in the *Not Me* category?

Like categorizing, labeling and comparisons also work against creating empowering self-beliefs. Labels are a quick and dirty way to categorize ourselves and others, often beginning in childhood and carried on into adulthood. Perhaps you unknowingly adopted a label others assigned to you. If you accept the label "Mathematically Challenged," for instance, anything related to math automatically goes in the *Not Me* category, and the label is difficult to shake. You might successfully solve math problems you encounter if you could simply get the limiting label out of the way.

Comparisons are an inaccurate way to decide if items fit into the *Me* or *Not Me* category. When you compare yourself to others, you likely focus on your deficits rather than on your strengths, making you feel inferior and incomplete. It is important to remember that people tend to present an edited version of their true selves to the outside world, which means you are comparing yourself to unrealistic standards. Take, for example, the Zen-like woman we used to admire in our yoga class. She seemed to have it all together. Unlike us, she looked so peaceful as she easily moved through the yoga poses. One day our friend, Angie, joined us for class and, to our surprise, knew this meditative maven from work. Angie later described her co-worker as easily frustrated and highly emotional. We had incorrectly ascribed to this woman a perfect life based solely on her yoga practice. Given the limited picture we see of others, we can easily overestimate the positive aspects of their lives.

Another risk of comparing yourself to others is assuming other people were born with the skills you admire, and you were not blessed with those abilities or attributes. The truth is that, although people have natural aptitudes and preferences, no one is a natural-born writer, tennis player, or cellist. People develop most skills over time with practice. We often doubt our ability to achieve something because people who are proficient at a task make it look deceptively easy. Without taking the time to explore the fundamentals of a skill, understand what is involved at this level of proficiency, or look at the beginner level of a task, you may believe the skill is mysterious and unattainable. Don't let this belief become an excuse for not trying to acquire a new skill! Our friend, Dave, refused to use this excuse and has become one of the most inspiring educators we know. He has spent countless hours developing creative ways to engage his students. When others comment that Dave's natural creativity made planning great lessons easy for him, it really irks him. In doing so, people simply dismiss the hard work and dedication he has given to his craft.

DO YOU KNOW THE TERRAIN?

We once worked with a new teacher who was in tears and on the verge of quitting. She determined she was a terrible and incompetent teacher because a lesson she taught had really bombed. She always heard the experienced teachers sharing fabulous lessons and ideas in the teachers' lounge and, when she visited their classrooms, she witnessed an engaged, productive atmosphere. These teachers seemed to have it all together, and she felt she could never be as competent as they were. Luckily, as she was sharing this, a wiser, more experienced, and very effective teacher came by and shared one of her own lessons which did not go as planned, to say the least. She assured the new teacher *all* teachers have similar moments, but over time, they develop strategies for course correcting when it's needed. No one is born a phenomenal teacher, but with reflection and practice, teachers can develop phenomenal teaching skills. An undeniable connection exists between confidence and competence. Because performance depends greatly upon your belief in your own ability, confidence directly impacts your performance. When you feel prepared for a test, you are more certain of the answers, and when you have practiced your speech, you deliver it with self-assurance. In the same way, your expectations of student learning depend largely upon your confidence in your own ability to teach. As school administrators, our expectations of teacher performance are closely tied to our confidence in our ability to lead. In the same way, teachers' expectations of student performance are closely related to their confidence in their ability to teach. Do ineffective teachers believe their kids can't learn, or are they deeply insecure about their ability to teach them? Undoubtedly, both are true. Successful educators know what they believe about themselves influences what they believe about students. These beliefs become a cycle: positively impacting students leads to greater teaching confidence, which leads to greater likelihood of positively impacting students. Confidence breeds competence, and competence breeds confidence.

CONFIDENCE BREEDS
COMPETENCE, AND
COMPETENCE BREEDS
CONFIDENCE.

The patterned stories you tell yourself can also inhibit the development of empowering self-beliefs. Perhaps you're holding yourself back with stories like: *I'm not good enough. My students can't do this. It's impossible.* Become aware of limiting stories and figure out why you keep telling them. Do they allow you to stay safely in your comfort zone and avoid the discomfort of change? Do they protect you from the potential embarrassment of making mistakes? Remember, what you focus on becomes your reality and, if you continue to tell these stories, you perpetuate your current reality.

Instead, choose to change your perceptions. Choose to focus on empowering stories and create the outcomes—the new reality—you desire. With awareness and practice, you can purposefully choose your thoughts and behavior. Again, never underestimate the big impact of making small changes over time. What we choose to do *daily* matters so much more than what we choose to do *occasionally*. Our friend, Kathy, says the daily choices she has made before and after work—getting enough sleep, eating breakfast, watching less television—have had the greatest positive impact on her teaching. But before she could make those changes, she first had to change her perceptions of herself. She had to tell herself she was worth it and change some limiting beliefs and patterns. As a result of those choices, Kathy became a more energized and effective teacher for her students.

The only way to consistently realize the outcomes we desire is to take responsibility for them. Attributing your outcomes to chance, luck, or outside influences allows you to stay safely in your comfort zone. Believing your actions don't matter gives you a reason to avoid trying. You have the ability—the *responsibility*—to own your choices and your outcomes, both the successes and the failures. Pay attention to the stories you tell yourself. Embrace empowering stories and discard limiting beliefs. Past failures and disappointments have no bearing on the future for you or your students if you truly believe in the power of possibility. Cultivate unwavering belief in yourself, and take bold steps in the direction of your goals. If your map is leading you to resist taking this ownership and action, it is time to revise your map.

Map-Changing Actions

Create a personal circle of concern. Draw two large circles on a piece of paper, one inside the other. In the outer circle, write all of the things troubling you over which you have no control. In the inner circle, write the things you are struggling about which you can control. Cut the two circles apart, and put the outer circle—the things you can't control—out of your sight. Focus only on the inside circle. Choose one or two items from the inside circle worthy of your time and effort, and then make a plan of action to improve them.

Map-Changing Questions

1. Think of your successes. Did they happen by chance or because of your choices?

2. Are you spending more effort and energy on things inside or outside of your control?

3. What would you need to do differently to feel more empowered and confident?

4. How would this impact your teaching and leading?

SHARE YOUR JOURNEY
WITH OTHER MAP
CHANGERS USING THE
#UNMAPPEDED HASHTAG.

Mapping Challenges as Opportunities

4

NOTHING CAN COMPARE TO THE TRAGEDY OF LOSING A STUDENT. Whether the loss is due to illness or accident, our hearts break. Zach Tucker is one of those students who left this world way too early. He was a healthy, happy second-grade boy playing kickball on the last day of school in June. But he was diagnosed with an aggressive form of cancer in July. The following May, after months of fighting the disease, Zach passed away. As difficult as this time was, we discovered some gifts hidden in the pain and challenge. Losing Zach put everything in perspective. His passing prompted us to reflect on how we were spending our time with students, and we began to really notice and appreciate each child in our care. Undeniably, we are better educators because of the students we have loved and lost.

We have also been inspired by Zach's family, who turned the incredible challenge of losing Zach into an opportunity to help others. When the holidays came, the Tucker family struggled with whether or not to hang Zach's stocking. They chose to hang the stocking and fill it with gift cards for other families coping with childhood cancer. That small act turned into a foundation that has provided support to over 650 families as of the writing of this book. The Tuckers continue to share their story of hope with others. The truth is that gifts and opportunities are found in all difficult situations and challenges. We just have to look past the pain to find them. Unfortunately, our tendency is to avoid challenge. All of us—young and old—want to feel safe, valued, competent, and capable. We also fear being ridiculed or shamed. As such, we avoid challenges in an effort to avoid discomfort, embarrassment, or criticism. However, there is no real growth without struggle, no gain without pain. Sometimes the biggest problem we (and our students) have is that we don't think we should have any problems. But we acquire the greatest learning—the kind we internalize and apply in different contexts—when things are hard.

DEALING WITH THE OBSTACLES IN YOUR PATH

We should not avoid or fear difficulties; in contrast, we should welcome them as a means to help us grow. Sometimes we experience challenges or frustrations because an area of our lives needs our attention, and we often come out on the other side of a challenge stronger than before. Our favorite coach, Tony, explained how muscles are strengthened when we exercise. Each time we push ourselves to the limit, further than we thought we could go, our muscles become damaged with tiny tears in the tissue. This is why we get sore after a tough workout. Muscle strengthening and growth is the result of our bodies repairing and fusing muscle fibers back together to form a stronger muscle. In the same way, our minds grow from working through challenges and, with enough effort, our potential is limitless.

With some biological exceptions, such as height or shoe size, we can improve almost all personal qualities with time and effort. We may have different starting points, but *we* determine our ending points. Psychologist and researcher Carol Dweck calls this a "growth mindset." People using a growth mindset are focused on learning and growing. They know perseverance leads to progress. Consider this formula for success:

$$\text{Ability x Effort} = \text{Success}$$

The less ability or inherent aptitude you have, the more effort you must apply. A growth mindset doesn't ignore differences in inherent aptitude, but those different starting points are unrelated to the ending point. What determines your success is your own willingness to do the work.

CLIMBING CLIFFS AND CANYONS

When you want to master something new, viewing it as a series of steps or skills can be helpful. You can break almost any task into levels of increasing complexity. For example, you had to learn to balance before you learned to walk, and you had to learn to walk before you learned to run. Certainly, no parent expects his baby to go from holding onto the coffee table to sprinting in perfect form in an afternoon. Similarly, you need time to work through every step of the process in order to master something new. For this reason, if you're learning from another person, it may be beneficial to seek a mentor who is just one step ahead of you in the process rather than someone with great expertise. People who are proficient make things look deceptively easy.

We are always amazed by the performances of our friend Jan's fifth-grade music students. She has taught many of these students since kindergarten and simply builds upon their skills every year—from keeping a steady beat to reading musical notes to playing the violin. Her students weren't born with musical talent, and they didn't develop talent overnight. But time and effort, along with purposeful scaffolding from Jan, produced their sweet-sounding musical mastery.

In contrast to a growth mindset, a *fixed mindset* implies we are born with a finite amount of a talent or ability. Therefore, we can't develop qualities we don't already have. Instead of applying effort to grow, people using a fixed mindset focus on areas where they have some natural aptitude, covering up areas where they don't. Notice we said people *use* a fixed mindset rather than people *have* a fixed mindset. The truth is, we all have a fixed mindset *and* a growth mindset, and we use both at one time or another. You can increase your use of a growth mindset through attention and practice, but the fixed mindset will still sneak in sometimes. The key is to notice it and deal with it. When do you notice your fixed mindset sneaking in?

Signs you are using a fixed mindset include feeling anxious, incompetent, or hopeless in the face of a challenge. You may begin to make excuses or become defensive. You may feel envious or threatened when you see someone do something better than you. When the fixed mindset sneaks in, don't deny it. Notice it, accept the feelings, and then attend to your thoughts. You can even name your fixed mindset like you did the negative voice in your head, especially since they are, in fact, the same. Just like you learned to do with the negative voice, question your fixed mindset, argue with it, and replace the limiting messages with more empowering messages. Try adding "yet" to any limiting statement. For example, *I am not a math person* becomes *I am not a math person yet*. "Yet" leaves room for endless possibilities and helps you focus on the growth mindset.

It's true that a growth mindset can be strengthened through attention and practice, but we would be doing you a disservice if we led you to believe a growth mindset is concerned only with effort and perseverance. Effort and perseverance are simply means to achieving a goal. Praising and celebrating effort is motivating, but it is not enough for growth. When the two of us were learning to play tennis, we could have invested an enormous amount of sweat equity but still been eternally poor tennis players. We also needed the expertise of our friend, Valerie, who showed us how to hold the racquet and move about the court. We needed her strategies and feedback to improve our game. Valerie could have just watched and yelled, "You girls are really working hard out there! Way to go!" We would have felt great! Our self-esteem might have been sky high—but our ranking at tennis tournaments would have been dreadfully low. Honoring our effort and celebrating progress keeps us motivated, but we also need to learn explicit strategies and receive specific feedback in order to maximize our potential.

When stuck in a fixed mindset, you may sidestep challenges in an effort to avoid criticism or negative feedback. But feedback is actually a gift, and the most helpful and encouraging feedback is tied to the process, not the person. Personal praise alone can make us fearful of doing anything to damage someone's initial assessment of our good qualities. It tugs at our need for self-preservation and makes us less likely to take risks. For example, if you write a beautiful piece for a blog and receive praise for being a gifted writer, you may feel anxious about living up to the acclaim the next time you write. On the other hand, if you are praised for the *thought and effort* reflected in your writing, you may feel motivated to take more risks as a writer, without the fear of damaging your reputation. The very best praise is both process focused and specific. It acknowledges effort and identifies exactly what was done well. If praised for the time and effort you put into your writing, as well as your effective use of verbs, you are pumped to step up and stretch further the next time.

Effective feedback also helps you see where you are in relation to your goal. Talking about needs and next steps can help you understand the time and effort required to reach the next level. This kind of feedback is based on performance and grounded in evidence. As principals tasked with giving tons of feedback, we've learned giving effective feedback can be challenging. We've found starting with a bit of specific praise primes the listener to focus on the areas needing improvement. Our friend, Kate, who supervises teaching interns at a college, has discovered the same thing. She describes the importance of positive feedback for these novice teachers but also acknowledges she sometimes has to work hard to give specific and authentic praise. One teacher's lesson she observed was really rough. Even so, she managed to affirm the teacher by saying, "You maximized instructional time when you turned quickly to the right page in the reading book," and this little nugget was enough to encourage a struggling intern as Kate helped her lay out a plan for improvement.

Feedback is critical, especially when things aren't going well. Struggling is part of growing, but failure and setbacks themselves don't lead to growth and change; they must be accompanied by reflection and learning. This ensures you don't waste your struggles and mistakes, but squeeze every bit of learning out of them. Math teacher and mindset expert, Eduardo Briceño, classifies mistakes into four categories—sloppy mistakes, high-stakes mistakes, stretch mistakes, and aha-moment mistakes—and proposes each kind of mistake leads to a different kind of learning.

Sloppy mistakes happen when we lose focus, rush through a task, or get distracted. Our friend, Ken, is an awesome dad who agonized over a sloppy mistake. Ken takes pride in packing lunches for his kids every day. One hectic morning, he got up late and handed a lunchbox to his daughter as she was running out the door. When she opened it at lunchtime, all she found was the sandwich crust and an empty pudding cup from the day before. Sloppy mistakes teach us, even though we may be proficient, that we still need to attend to the task at hand. They can also warn us to take better care of ourselves since we often make them when we are tired or hungry. Sloppy mistakes affirm that we really can't multi-task (which has been scientifically proven) and need to turn off our devices or better arrange our schedules and work spaces.

High-stakes mistakes occur when outcomes have a big impact on the future. Likely, we can all recall at least one player whose high-stakes mistake blew a big game for our favorite team. These mistakes happen at summative or culminating events, such as a final exam or state championship game. Events like these teach us to deal with pressure and anxiety. They teach us to deal with great and not-so-great outcomes, with victory and defeat. High-stakes mistakes are often public and painful, but they can be catalysts for big growth.

Stretch mistakes happen when we decide to try something well beyond the scope of our current abilities. These mistakes are purposeful because we are stretching to learn something new and understand we are likely to make mistakes in the process. For example, a child learning to ride a bicycle knows she is likely to make a wrong move and fall off the bike but keeps trying anyway. If you really want to break out of your comfort zone, stretch mistakes are the way to go.

Aha-moment mistakes occur when we do something we intend to but, in the process, discover surprising new information. Aha-moment mistakes are powerful because they lead to an unexpected insight or discovery, catapulting our growth. Sometimes, the *aha* is discovering a task is more nuanced or complex than we initially realized, while other times it is suddenly seeing the solution to a persistent problem. At the end of *The Wizard of Oz*, Dorothy realized she failed in her efforts to get home to Kansas. At this moment of failure, Glenda, the good witch, helped her make a discovery: She always had the power. Dorothy's *aha* moment came when she realized she had the ability to get home all along—she simply needed to click the heels of her ruby red shoes together!

When you try to avoid the struggle of a challenge or escape the consequences of a mistake, you cheat yourself out of an opportunity to grow. We have both tried to convince a teacher to persist through a difficult situation rather than giving up, often when relationships with students or parents become strained. While we understand teachers might ask for an especially difficult student to be moved from their class in order to avoid further angst or discomfort, this sends a message to the student she is not worthy of the effort and also robs the teacher of an opportunity to add to his toolbox.

WHEN YOU TRY TO AVOID THE STRUGGLE OF A CHALLENGE OR ESCAPE THE CONSEQUENCES OF A MISTAKE, YOU CHEAT YOURSELF OUT OF AN OPPORTUNITY TO GROW.

Jenny is an amazing teacher who experienced this situation. One of her students had some challenging behaviors, which seemed to be growing more and more frequent and disruptive. The student's parent was becoming frustrated as well, evident in daily notes to Jenny, which seemed combative. Jenny finally came to the office, close to tears, and asked for the student to be moved to another class. After we talked to her about the message this would send, the potential impact the move might have on her colleagues, and the support we could offer, she decided to continue trying to work with the student. With time, effort, and interventions developed with the school counselor, the student began to improve. Jenny often says she is a much better teacher for sticking with the student through the rough patch, and, certainly, her efforts profoundly impacted the future of the child.

YOUR MAP AS A MODEL

By cultivating growth mindsets, we model these practices for our students. When they see us react positively to mistakes, they receive messages about our beliefs. When we acknowledge our own mistakes and learn from them, students notice. When we reflect and adjust, we model a growth mindset. Focusing on our own growth as educators not only pays big dividends for us—it benefits our students as well.

Living without making a mistake is impossible. So how will you choose to react to your mistakes? Operating from a growth mindset and learning from mistakes ensures progress and improvement. When you embrace mistakes as tools for growth, you take risks. When you take risks, you continue to grow. Putting a pattern of risk-taking and reflection on your map makes any problem or challenge a potential gift or opportunity.

Map-Changing Actions

Use visualization to grow in competence and confidence. Visualizing is powerful because our brains experience real and imagined actions in the same way. Therefore, the more you "practice" a task through visualization, the more successful you will be when you perform it. When you repeatedly visualize successfully performing a task, you create neural pathways that make the action feel familiar when you have to perform it in a real context.

Close your eyes and see yourself successfully performing something challenging, whether it is a lesson you will teach or a difficult conversation you need to have with a student. Imagine the event in vivid detail. Imagine the sensory details—what you see, hear and feel—as you perform the task. Envisioning your state may also be helpful. For example, seeing yourself in a calm state may decrease physical symptoms of stress when the time comes to perform it. Finally, envisioning success can enhance motivation and confidence, making you more likely to continue despite challenges.

Map-Changing Questions

1. What do you try to hide from others when you want to make a good impression?

2. How can you shift your focus from what others think about you to your own improvement or growth?

3. How do you tend to respond to feedback and criticism?

4. How do you tend to react when you make a mistake?

5. How could you better use mistakes and challenges as vehicles for growth?

SHARE YOUR JOURNEY WITH OTHER MAP CHANGERS USING THE #UNMAPPEDED HASHTAG.

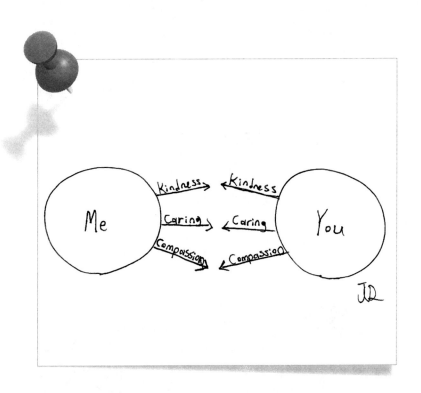

5
Your Map Impacts Others

A T ANY GIVEN MOMENT, YOU CAN BE AN ENERGY *BOOST* (CULTIVATING POSITIVITY AND PASSION THAT REFRESHES AND RENEWS OTHERS) OR AN ENERGY *DRAIN* (UNLOADING NEGATIVITY AND ANGST, AND LITERALLY SUCKING THE LIFE OUT OF A ROOM). Peaches was an energy *boost*. Before automated toll roads, Peaches (that was the name on her nametag) worked in a tollbooth near our town. Every day, regardless of how busy the road was, Peaches would greet each driver with authentic enthusiasm, sincerely complimenting a new coffee mug, earrings, or the baby in the backseat. Each driver felt certain he was Peaches' favorite customer and, no matter how the day had started, he drove away feeling better.

Don't we want our students and their parents to feel this way after spending time with us? Your positivity and passion reflect your beliefs. And the energy you give to others comes back to you. Your beliefs about others largely determine how you interact with them, and the way you interact with others—and make them *feel*—largely determines how they respond to you. If you pay attention, you will see others are constantly giving you feedback regarding the signals you are sending. Rather than just reacting to those around you, you can learn from them and purposefully adjust what you are communicating.

THE ENERGY YOU GIVE TO OTHERS COMES BACK TO YOU.

DO YOU HAVE ENOUGH FUEL FOR THE JOURNEY?

As an energy *booster*, your positive feelings toward others must be sincere. You cannot fake warm regard and caring; your subtleties will always give you away. People respond to your energy and nonverbal cues. They can sense how you feel about them regardless of what you say. Scientist and author Jill Bolte Taylor wrote about suffering a stroke in the left hemisphere of her brain, causing the temporary loss of the logical, analytical left-brain functions. With the intuitive right brain dominating, she became attuned to the energy people brought into her hospital room. She responded to the subtle, nonverbal ways of showing love by those who were gentle, caring, and attentive. Similarly, those we teach and lead intuitively respond to the energy we bring into our classrooms and schools. If we really want to change the way others respond to us, we have to look deeply into the beliefs influencing our energy.

You send out a multitude of subtle signals every minute, ultimately giving away your true feelings. In order to fake a feeling, you would have to consciously control everything from vocal fluctuations to the position of your shoulders to the tension around your eyes. Even a highly effective poker player can't do that. You simply cannot micromanage all the tiny movements indicating how you feel. When you put on a smile to "fake it till you make it," eventually a microexpression—a fleeting movement of facial muscles—will flash across your face and give your true feelings away. Studies have shown people can read facial expressions lasting only seventeen milliseconds and can accurately differentiate between a fake smile and a true one, based solely on the corners of one's eyebrows. Your thoughts are literally written all over your face. The physical expression of your thoughts on your face and in your body language inevitably and reliably reveal to others what is on your mind.

WATCH THE GAUGES (BE SURE YOU'RE READING THEM CORRECTLY)

Your struggle to connect with some people is likely rooted in your thoughts about them. Chances are, you think about them as problems to be managed rather than as people with needs as important as your own. Author Tony Morrison once said the key to parenting was making sure your eyes light up when your children walk into the room. She knew children sense whether we are happy to see them or aggravated by their presence, and they respond accordingly. When you are detectably annoyed by someone, they will likely sense it and may react with anger or withdrawal—a response that likely increases your irritation. Ironically, when you view others as annoyances, you risk provoking the very behavior you complain about.

Kristin, a fellow principal, told us about a teacher she had difficulty connecting with because he seemed unable to detect the needs of others or read their signals, and he caused much dissention on his team. He would often circle the school office or another teacher's space until the teacher or administrator answered his question or met his need. Once, during a difficult conversation, he expressed he wanted to have the same kind of relationship with Kristen as other staff members had with her. She realized while she hadn't meant to treat him differently, she was less than excited to see him every day and had been sending signals accordingly. Kristen had to make a conscious effort to view him with compassion and understand his needs so he could feel her warm regard and caring. Amazingly, once she changed the way she viewed him, his behavior started to change as well. We all have students or colleagues who challenge us. If we focus on changing our thoughts about them, we can improve our relationships with them.

Your own fear and insecurity can cause you to view others in a negative way, which, in turn, can make them feel fearful and insecure. When there is a conflict, it is human nature to justify your actions or inactions. Remember, your brain seeks to preserve your positive self-image. You can easily minimize your faults and maximize your virtue. Likewise, you may inflate another's faults and diminish her virtue. The two of us hate to admit we have sometimes blamed students for their own choices instead of acknowledging our failure to provide what they needed. While we can easily become frustrated when students are off task or disengaged, we have to take responsibility for our part, especially if it is due to our own disengagement or lack of planning.

It is possible to create conflict without any help from others, often stemming from guilt we feel about our own action or inaction. We justify situations to escape these feelings of guilt. For example, if you and I are assigned to lunch duty, but I frequently choose not to go, I likely feel guilty for sticking you with all the responsibility. But I don't want to feel guilty, so when I see you, I attribute any perceived lack of friendliness on your part to your issues, instead of to my letting you down. My mental conversation goes like this: "She is so judgmental! She has no idea how much I have going on. I hope I don't get stuck having duty with her again next semester." So our own feelings and perceptions of others may actually be tied to how we have treated them, rather than to anything they have done to us. Ignoring what we know is right creates self-justifying beliefs. When we know what we should do, and choose not to do it, we damage relationships.

BE AWARE OF THE WARNING SIGNS

Conflict can also arise from the many patterns you've likely developed to protect your ego. You are probably unaware of how often you use them. For example, when I feel defensive, I need you to be wrong so I can be right. Likewise, I blame others because of my own insecurities, not necessarily because of their actions or inactions. We never blame with the intention of helping others. We blame to protect our own fragile self-images, and it causes others to become defensive, inviting a continuation of the very problem for which we are blaming them. By contrast, if we accept our own responsibility and solve a problem with the intention of helping others, this can help to reduce conflict. What ego protecting patterns do you find yourself using?

You do not need to excuse the unacceptable or inappropriate behavior of others. However, you can choose to avoid laying blame and focus on problem-solving to ease, rather than escalate, a difficult situation. Our friend and guidance counselor, Marcie, demonstrated this when she had to settle a conflict between a teacher and a parent who was upset because her child earned a poor grade on a homework assignment. The student claimed he did not understand the assignment, the parent blamed the teacher for not explaining it clearly, and the teacher blamed the student for not listening to directions. The argument went round and round until Marcie focused everyone on helping the student learn and grow. Then they were able to work together productively.

Another suggestion for avoiding conflict and boosting relationship energy is to identify ineffective behaviors or practices without judging the person. Criticize the action instead of the character of the actor. To do this, sincerely view the person as capable of improving given time and practice. If the other person senses judgment creeping in, the honesty and transparency regarding his own actions will likely cease. If he knows he should have done something differently, he will likely justify his behavior by projecting negative characteristics onto you. As principals, the two of us have often been tasked with helping teachers improve instructional practices. If we had communicated in a judgmental way, the teachers would have surely become defensive. In that case, they would have clammed up and left the office feeling an unfair leader was picking on them. Focusing on the instruction, rather than the instructor, allowed us to have the open, honest, and reflective dialogue necessary for growth.

When you understand people act on the outside the way they feel on the inside, it is easier to be patient with them. Compassion is a sense of shared suffering accompanied by a desire to help. You can practice compassion by recognizing the feelings of others and looking for your similarities rather than your differences. This is difficult to do when someone treats you with disrespect, but if you can see the hurt behind the behavior, you can truly respond with compassion. Compassion requires the willingness to understand the other person's point of view, even when you do not agree. As teachers and leaders, we may find ourselves on the receiving end of displaced aggression, and we may be tempted to respond in kind.

Our friend and fellow principal, Jesse, experienced this with a grandmother who needed compassion, even if she did not seem to deserve it. Her grandson had made an inappropriate choice and earned a consequence. When the grandmother called to disagree, vehemently and disrespectfully, she threatened Jesse with a call to the superintendent. The grandmother extended the invitation and, unfortunately, Jesse accepted it. She participated in the argument by replying, "Get a pen so I can tell you what to tell the superintendent about your grandson." This was not a proud moment, and her choice only escalated the situation. Listening and responding with compassion surely would have brought a better outcome.

Accepting invitations to respond with unkindness is tempting, but that can escalate and complicate a situation. Instead, you can choose to decline these invitations, hold your peace, and give respect even when it is not earned. By doing so, you ultimately prevail because you will likely regret being angry, but you will never regret being kind.

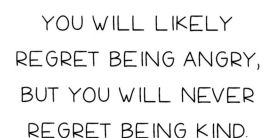

YOU WILL LIKELY
REGRET BEING ANGRY,
BUT YOU WILL NEVER
REGRET BEING KIND.

Another way to be an energy *boost* is by avoiding assumptions regarding others' intentions. The best way to challenge these assumptions is to state them and then add the word *maybe*. For example, if you are tempted to say, "She is faking illness to get out of working on the fundraiser," tack on a *maybe*. "She is faking illness to get out of working on the fundraiser—maybe" sends the message to yourself there might be another explanation. Thinking, "He is only taking on additional responsibility to impress the superintendent," may or may not be his true intention. Adding *maybe* makes room in your mind for other possibilities; it opens up a path for understanding and compassion.

LET KINDNESS BE YOUR GUIDE

Your greatest investment as an educator is your relationships with students. As noted above, the nonverbal signals you give will have a greater impact on these relationships than anything you say to your students. Do your eyes light up when students walk into your classroom? Are you genuinely happy to see them? Do you view them as people with needs as important as your own? You can try to fake it, but even young students are highly intuitive. Your subtleties will always give you away. Because your responses to students may be influenced by their appearance, behavior, social class, and race, you must take time to get to know each student so you can build rapport and trust with them.

When your students feel you value and care for them as individuals, they are more to likely to comply with your requests. When you are respectful and kind, students appreciate you. When they appreciate you, they want to please you—which means they are more likely to meet your expectations. When it comes to student behavior, relationships trump rules every time. So developing relationships should be the most important component of your discipline plan. When you have to correct a student, do so privately when you are in control of your own emotions. You can listen and validate the student's feelings while firmly maintaining high expectations.

When evaluating the relationships part of your map, take the time to honestly assess and adjust the way you view others. Your subtle cues will always indicate what is on your map. Those you teach and lead can clearly sense how you feel about them, and they respond accordingly. Freely give kindness and compassion, and it will come back to you. As an educator, you are in a position to help others grow, and you can only facilitate growth when you truly believe it is possible. When you approach others with warmth and caring, while still challenging them to rise, you assemble a host of loyal collaborators on this journey.

Map-Changing Actions

Visualize someone who is challenging to you. Consider the first thoughts you have when you encounter this person. Now consider the person's needs and challenges as well as her hopes and desires. Cultivate compassionate thoughts by trying to understand her perspective and sincerely intending to help. Visualize a ray of light from the center of your body connecting to a light from the other person and focus on the connection. Thinking of yourself as connected to others—rather than separated from them—facilitates compassion and kindness. Your new way of responding to this person might just reduce the very behavior frustrating you.

Map-Changing Questions

1. How does the energy you bring into your classroom and school impact others?

2. How are your thoughts and beliefs impacting your relationships?

3. How do those you teach and lead know you care for them?

4. In what ways can you invest in better relationships?

SHARE YOUR JOURNEY
WITH OTHER MAP
CHANGERS USING THE
#UNMAPPEDED HASHTAG.

Fear   Faith
↓   ↓
Control   Vs.   Choice
↓   ↓
Disengagement   Engagement

6
Prospecting for Potential

WE ARE BOTH MOTHERS OF BOYS WHO WEAR GLASSES. When Connor, Julie's son, was a high school freshman, his driver's education teacher discovered he had less-than-perfect eyesight. The eye doctor confirmed he would indeed be a hazard behind the wheel, so this fifteen-year-old got some glasses. Connor was very self-conscious about wearing his new glasses to school, but luckily, his aunt was a teacher at the high school he attended. "So many kids wear glasses," she told him. "Tomorrow, I want you to count all of the kids you see with glasses." When he came home that day, he shared that almost a third of the students in his school wore them. He couldn't understand why he never noticed before. Undoubtedly, he noticed kids wearing glasses because he was looking for kids wearing glasses.

One thing is certain about beliefs and expectations: you find what you look for. If you look for problems and deficits in your students, you will find them. If you look for gifts and strengths, you will find them. Thanks to an overabundance of data, we know more about the deficits and strengths of our students than we ever did before. But why do we immediately zoom in on the weaknesses? This laser-like focus on remediation seems to drive many of our current policies and practices. But perhaps we are misusing data in a very important way. You see, data only shows where a student was at *one point in time.* Data cannot possibly paint a picture of what the student will be in the future. Journalist Malcolm Gladwell stated, "A prediction in a field where prediction is not possible is no more than a prejudice." If our mental maps are leading us to focus on where a student has been as an indication of where the student is headed, then we need to revise our maps. Let's choose to focus on a powerful vision for each student's future success. Instead of just mining for minimal mastery, let's start prospecting for potential.

WHERE IS YOUR FOCUS?

The two of us have visited persistently low-achieving schools where teachers and leaders often talk about the overwhelming task of bringing so many low-performing students up to minimal grade-level standards. When we suggest what they really have is an abundance of students with untapped potential, we are typically met with stunned silence. Moving from a focus on deficits to a focus on capacity is a big paradigm shift—a shift requiring us to see the great challenges our students have overcome as evidence of their potential, rather than evidence of their vulnerability.

Muhammad Ali understood this paradigm shift. Born in the segregated southern town of Louisville, Kentucky, in 1942, he grew up battling racism, discrimination, and a series of intimidating opponents in the boxing ring. While many likely assumed a successful future for Ali was impossible, he believed the opposite: "Impossible is not a fact. It's an opinion. Impossible is not a declaration. It's a dare. Impossible is potential. Impossible is temporary. Impossible is nothing." Are you limiting yourself and your students with your beliefs about what is possible?

Focusing on weaknesses leads to a lack of student confidence, which leads to disengagement, which leads to inhibited learning. And when student learning is lagging, the cycle starts again with a focus on weaknesses. This disengagement-remediation cycle is difficult to break. In contrast, a strengths-based approach is built on a foundation of hope and optimism. The underlying philosophy is students already have strengths, abilities, and resources they can use to get through challenges. A strengths-based philosophy is grounded in appreciating the dignity, potential, rights, and individuality of each student. As such, resources are distributed with the intention of building upon strengths, rather than remediating deficits.

Students dealing with adversity have big potential for growth. Their challenges can become opportunities for greater wisdom and resilience, but they need help framing them this way. Building upon their strengths boosts students' confidence, engages them in learning, and maximizes growth. Students' academic achievement and emotional well-being significantly impact one another. Many students have considerable needs to address, but those are not the primary focus in a strengths-based classroom or school. Instead, remediation happens in the context of relevant and challenging work.

To prospect for potential, you must lose the labels. Labeling students can lead to assumptions and generalizations. Labels like *minority, disadvantaged,* and *low achieving* may automatically influence your expectations of your students and limit the options you see for them. Additionally, labels may negatively influence your students' expectations and limit the possibilities they see for themselves. It is imperative we question our assumptions and take the time to learn about each student as an individual, rather than generalizing because of a label. Our friend, Bernardo, teaches a diversity class to preservice teachers. One of their assignments is to use a mock roster to plan accommodations for English Language Learners. Initially, these future teachers plan the same general accommodations for the whole group, and Bernardo has to point out the students on the roster are at different levels of proficiency in English as well as different levels of literacy in their home languages. He enjoys seeing the aspiring teachers realize the ELL label does not mean all of them have the same needs.

Labels make it easy to attribute student disengagement to a lack of ability or motivation, when disengagement often results from a lack of confidence. After successive failures, some students feel helpless and give up. But all students need a challenging and relevant curriculum,

> LABELS MAKE IT EASY TO ATTRIBUTE STUDENT DISENGAGEMENT TO A LACK OF ABILITY OR MOTIVATION, WHEN DISENGAGEMENT OFTEN RESULTS FROM A LACK OF CONFIDENCE.

regardless of their current achievement level—and struggling students need it most of all. In fact, tying curriculum to students' personal experiences increases their confidence. Students bring cultural capital and skills teachers can build on, affirming and validating their strengths. Let students start with what they know and what they can do, then gently push them to go further. Building students' capacity is an ongoing process, not a short-term fix. If students spend most of their time memorizing, recalling, and filling in blanks, they will find little value in school. However, if students have opportunities to engage in conversations and assignments, allowing them to explore important issues and solve real problems, they will find meaning. The best lessons create a bridge between school and students' lives, and this home-school connection boosts motivation and confidence.

Prospecting for potential also means giving choice and a voice to all students, especially those who have experienced challenges. Unfortunately, the reverse often happens. Teachers often give students who struggle less freedom, and the omission of choice and voice is a clear indication of low expectations. Belief in a person's potential is inversely related to the need for control. People remove choice and autonomy when they do not trust someone's ability to make good choices for himself. In the same way, educators who don't trust their students' abilities often become overly directive. Their control might show up in the form of overly scripted lessons with little room for interaction or in narrow assignments with little room for differentiation. It may also come in the removal of arts and enrichment opportunities. Control can often come from fear—perhaps fear of an inability to reach and teach your students, fear about the students' inability to perform, or fear about how others might judge you. But control isn't a solution; taking away choice and voice and replacing them with overprescribed requirements limits potential.

Another challenge to supporting student choice and voice relates to high-stakes tests, which can become a major source of fear for both teachers and students. Standardized tests narrowly define learning and ignore the dynamic and complex characteristics of learners. The way you talk about assessments and test scores creates the reality for your students and impacts the way they internalize their results, so choose your words very carefully. Students must hear messages reaffirming they are more than their test scores and their learning is much broader than what a single score could represent. After all, test scores are just a small piece of a big, complex, and dynamic puzzle.

The misuse of data also creates fear, which leads to control rather than choice and voice. Relying on quantitative data alone gives a myopic view of student success. Numerical scores can help you see trends, but numbers will never tell you *why*. For example, data from a recent reading test might indicate all of your third graders struggled with a certain test item, but the only way to know *why* each child struggled is to sit alongside them and ask why each picked the answer she picked. Talking with students in this way—also known as *qualitative data gathering*—is powerful. Students present a deeper picture of their thinking in their own words. Defining yourself and your students by singular, narrow measures of success is limiting. A much bigger picture more accurately represents your students' and your work.

The two of us used this kind of qualitative data collection when preparing this chapter. We talked to educators and students and observed practices in schools. For example, we asked students in the schools we visited what happened in their classrooms that made them feel smart. The students said they felt smart when their teachers knew their names, made eye contact, smiled, and talked about things important to them. They also said interesting and challenging lessons gave them clues their teacher cared about and believed in them. Again, as teachers and leaders, we must be aware of the subtle messages our instructional choices and actions send to students. Mundane tasks and humdrum lessons send messages of low expectations.

Differences in teaching practices between higher- and lower-performing students only widen the achievement gap. For example, we observed inconsistencies in the relevance and rigor of assignments, with teachers often assigning struggling students less difficult and less pertinent tasks. If students go through the motions of learning without knowing what and why they are learning, they will not engage. Furthermore, going through the motions never results in big learning gains. In addition to better quality assignments, higher-performing students often received superior and more detailed feedback on their work than struggling students did, which is unfortunate since the lower-performing students need quality feedback to build competence and confidence.

Differences in the manner and amount of time teachers spent interacting with higher- and lower-performing students was also apparent. The way teachers ask questions and involve students in discussions sends subtle, yet powerful, messages about expectations. High-achieving students tend to be called on more frequently than struggling students, and they are asked more challenging questions. Teachers also tend to stick with high performers longer, restating, prompting, and scaffolding them to the correct answer. One struggling student described a classroom practice called "phoning a friend," where students could ask other students for help answering questions. He explained, "The smart kids don't get to 'phone a friend.' The teacher lets us 'phone a friend' when she knows we can't figure out the answer." His teacher did not realize the message this practice was sending to this little learner.

The way teachers group students for instruction also sends messages about expectations. When the two of us visit schools, we often ask students about reading, and almost every single student frames his reading competence in terms of which reading group he is in. Students explain they are "good" readers because they are in the highest reading group or "bad" readers because they are in the low reading group. Simply assigning a student to a group or class can influence both teacher and student expectations and become a self-fulfilling prophecy. Ability grouping can also lead teachers to over-generalize regarding student needs. For example, two students may be reading on the same level and placed in the same reading group, indicating their needs are identical. However, if one struggles with phonics while the other struggles with comprehension, their needs are actually quite different.

WHAT ARE YOUR EXPECTATIONS?

We also talked to middle school and high school students who provided more insight into subtle ways teachers communicate their expectations. They said high-level math and science classes tend to emphasize inquiry, problem-solving, and cooperative work, while lower level classes focus on memorization, basic skills, and test preparation. Due to this structure, higher-level classes gave students a greater opportunity to be engaged in meaningful learning. These students also indicated teachers of these higher-level classes tended to be more enthusiastic and passionate, qualities that students view as indicators of high expectations. If we want to close the achievement gap, we must first close the opportunity gap. When we limit opportunities to learn, we limit potential.

Likely, the opportunity gap is created, in part, from sincere efforts to help lower-performing students. Unfortunately, behaviors intended to help struggling students often do the most harm. For example, letting students off the hook and protecting them from grappling with a challenge is an indication of low expectations—not a way to make learning easier for students. And while empathy is important, pity and sympathy have a negative impact on learning. Students also interpret general praise, such as "good job," given for an easy task as a sign of low expectations. Teachers may unintentionally give other harmful verbal clues, such as the one we once heard a teacher say, "Wow, Joey! I didn't think you would be able to do that problem!" Words she intended to be kind and encouraging turned out to be discouraging. Be mindful of your words and your actions. They both communicate your expectations of students.

WHEN WE LIMIT OPPORTUNITIES TO LEARN, WE LIMIT POTENTIAL.

Having a positive relationship with your students is a critical component of communicating high expectations. Positive student-teacher relationships improve a student's behavior, confidence, peer relationships, willingness to take risks, and amount of effort—and all of these factors impact student achievement. Strategies like a daily check-in, asking about students' interests, and actively listening can build stronger relationships. Caring and supporting do not mean lowering expectations. Tell students you believe in them and gently push them to achieve more. They will work hard to show your belief is justified. Students thrive in authentic relationships with adults based on unconditional caring and unwavering belief. How do your students know how much you care?

Our friend, Debbie, teaches a STEM class for students identified as gifted, and we love to visit her classroom where students are often engaged in exploratory, self-directed projects and investigations. Debbie knows and values each student's strengths and strives to create learning opportunities bridging those unique interests and abilities with math and science standards. Debbie is a great example for all of us. What would happen if we all treated our students as Debbie does—like gifted students? After all, each one *does have* unique gifts and talents. How would our classrooms and schools be different if we believed in the unlimited intellectual capacity of all students?

We must believe in the unlimited potential of our students—regardless of the neighborhoods or families they come from and regardless of their past performance. And we must communicate our belief through our words, actions, instructional decisions, and daily practices. Students are sophisticated observers, constantly making interpretations about our expectations and beliefs. Let's provide challenge in the context of care and support. Let's treat all students as if they are gifted—because they are. A strengths-based classroom is characterized by clear and consistent high expectations regarding work performance, attitudes, and behavior. Holding high expectations, while providing support, fosters student confidence. And as confidence increases, competence increases. If your map places limits on your students' abilities, your map is limiting their growth. It's time to cast a vision of limitless potential on your map.

Map-Changing Actions

You've heard about people going through life wearing rose-colored glasses. What if you entered your school or classroom each day wearing "strengths finder" goggles? What you look for, you will find, so why not look for the good in others? To spot their strengths, look for moments when they are excited about what they are saying or doing. Ask them what activities make them feel their best or most fulfilled. Take mental notes about what makes those you teach and lead shine, then find opportunities for them to shine more often.

Map-Changing Questions

1. What do you know about your students' strengths?

2. How can you build on their strengths and gently push them further?

3. What forms of evidence can allow your students to show what they know?

4. What do your current instructional practices communicate to students about your expectations?

SHARE YOUR JOURNEY WITH OTHER MAP CHANGERS USING THE #UNMAPPEDED HASHTAG.

Motivation on the Map

7

A S YOU BEGIN THIS CHAPTER, WE NEED TO GIVE YOU A WARNING. We are going to use a word some people find offensive: *sucks*. If you are one of those people, we apologize in advance. While it's not our favorite word either, no other word really fits. We can't talk about efficacy and effort without talking about the *Sucks-to-Value Ratio* (S:V)—the more we value something, the more we will endure what sucks about it. Our friend, Michael, a high school math teacher and assistant football coach, had a student who gave maximum effort on the football field but slacked off in math class. At football practice, the student hustled and did practice drills until the lights were shut off, but he never did his math homework. Michael wondered how this kid could put so much effort into football yet put so little into his education. We explained it's all about the *Sucks-to-Value Ratio*. His player loved football and was willing to endure what sucked about it. Unfortunately, he didn't seem to feel the same way about math class.

Our job as educators is not to make our classes easier; our job is to help students see the value in applying themselves. Our job is to show students that with time and effort, they can achieve a big goal. As with other goals, the path to reaching a learning goal isn't always fun, but students will work hard if they believe it's worth it.

GOING THE DISTANCE

In order to maximize student learning, both teacher efficacy and student efficacy must exist. Efficacy is comprised of two parts: the belief an outcome is possible and the belief one has the capacity (given enough time and practice) to achieve the outcome. Confidence covers the second part. Millionaire and maven Beyoncé, the queen of confidence, once said, "I don't like to gamble, but if there's one thing I'm willing to bet on, it's myself." Our students' success depends on our willingness to bet on them and our ability to convince them to bet on themselves. As our kids grow in confidence, they will also grow in competence. The same is true for us. As we strengthen our belief in our own abilities, we will become better teachers and leaders.

The level of self-confidence your students possess influences the height of the goals they set as well as their level of commitment to reaching those goals. You can start the ball rolling by setting goals *with* your students, not *for* your students. Being handed a predetermined goal creates the perception students have to prove themselves to you, and trying to prove ability while stretching for a lofty goal can lead to feelings of inadequacy. The gap between a student's current performance and the imposed target may seem daunting. Don't misunderstand. We're not saying you should set easily attainable goals. Those just communicate low expectations. We are suggesting you have honest conversations with each student about where she currently stands and then set a goal together. The target should be just beyond a student's reach—attainable, but requiring a stretch. The focus is then on *improving* rather than proving.

Next, identify data students can track and measure themselves. When used in this way, data can contribute to motivation and facilitate student ownership of their learning. Focus on tracking progress and growth, rather than on making comparisons with others or peak performance. For example, a student might develop this goal with you: "I will be able to complete forty out of fifty multiplication facts on a timed test at the end of the quarter—twice as many as I can do now." Since this is quite different than focusing on getting an A or the top score in the class, a motivated student will consistently practice each week, assess her own progress, and determine how far she still has to go to reach her goal. What data could you use to increase student ownership and motivation?

For better or worse, students' levels of confidence are often informed by comparisons. As we shared earlier, the most confident readers tend to be those who identify themselves as being in the highest reading group. Comparisons might work for the highest achiever, but they are confidence killers for struggling students. Students who struggle need to focus on individual data and growth instead. A classroom culture based on celebrating growth, regardless of individual rankings, is an environment ripe for building everyone's confidence.

Our friend, Rhonda, teaches students with exceptional needs, and all of her kids struggle with some aspects of reading. At her school, students earn points for taking computer-based quizzes on books they read. At the end of each grading period, the school rewards the students with the highest points, and the most coveted reward is lunch with the principal. Rhonda's students had never won. In fact, the same students received the reward every time. She realized that students can't feel like winners if they've never had a chance to win. So Rhonda proposed a revision to the plan, which was eventually accepted by the rest of the faculty. In the new plan, every student who meets his goal can enter into a drawing for the rewards. After she explained the new plan to her students, she witnessed a stronger sense of motivation as they read more books than ever before. Before long, one of her students' names was drawn for lunch with the principal, and this kicked up the motivation factor even more for all the students as they worked to meet their goals.

STUDENTS CAN'T FEEL LIKE WINNERS IF THEY'VE NEVER HAD A CHANCE TO WIN.

PAVING THE WAY FOR SUCCESS

How will you help your students develop the self-confidence they need to reach those stretch goals? Confidence is mainly informed by past successes. So students who don't have a history of academic success often feel insecure. You can help students develop self-confidence by allowing them to experience a sense of accomplishment through carefully sequencing and scaffolding tasks meant to improve their skills. When students have little or no experience in an area, your modeling can give them a starting point. Watching you demonstrate, while explicitly describing the necessary steps, helps students think about their own abilities in relation to the task. Relating new content or an unfamiliar task to something they already know can also give students the initial boost they need. Modeling, scaffolding, guiding, and accommodating students until their skills are strengthened enhances confidence. But beware of over-helping. Self-confidence only grows when students perceive tasks as challenging and when they complete these tasks with some degree of independence. Extremely easy tasks, or ones done with too much assistance, yield no confidence gains.

Achievements only impact confidence when students recognize them—so celebrate their successes. And celebrate them in ways students can recall when they need a boost. While there are at least a thousand ways to celebrate success with your students, these are some of our favorites:

- Send a *happy gram* or *positive phone call home.* These are traditional rewards but very effective.

- If you are a bit more techie, *Tweet* about it.

- Give a *pencil*—or better yet, a *Smencil*! These are small but meaningful gestures.

- Award the *special seat*—always a favorite. Our kids would sell a vital organ to sit in the rolling chair!

- Applaud with different kinds of claps—like the golf clap or the "round" of applause.

- Perform a few minutes of *All Star* on the karaoke machine (our personal favorite!). Who doesn't want to hear his teacher singing some Smash Mouth?

The possibilities are endless, and students always appreciate having a choice in their celebration.

Another way to build confidence in your students is to help them minimize anxious situations. A former deodorant commercial offers some sage advice: "Never let them see you sweat." Different physical states give us signals about our level of confidence, and when students are sweating or shaking, they judge themselves as less confident and less capable. Signs of anxiety can greatly impact performance. Anxious students can benefit from practicing relaxation techniques, such as deep breathing. Anxiety is directly related to uncertainty, so any information you can provide about an upcoming challenge is helpful. The more students know about what to expect, the lower their levels of anxiety.

Our friend, Kristi, was asked to lead a professional-development session at a district event. She was expecting a small group and planned an informal talk. However, when she arrived, nearly one hundred participants, including the superintendent and district staff, sat in the audience. She felt the unwelcome flutter of butterflies in her stomach. When she began to speak, she noticed that her voice seemed high pitched and shaky. Kristi completely forgot everything she planned to say. The unexpected crowd and her own signs of anxiety negatively impacted her performance.

Preparing our students well is essential to their success, and celebrating that success increases their confidence. But as teachers and leaders, we can leverage another confidence booster: pride. When students are proud to be part of a group and proud of their collective accomplishments, self-confidence increases. Pride shapes students' identities, increases their sense of belonging, and positively impacts self-esteem. To foster pride in your school or classroom, invite others in to see the students' work. Catch students making good choices (but tell them it doesn't surprise you). Brag about them to others loud enough so they can hear. One of our favorite first grade teachers, Bev, takes her students to the music classroom each week and, while dropping them off, tells the music teacher how well they follow directions. She follows the statement with a prediction about how much the music teacher is going to enjoy having them for the next hour. The music teacher notices these students work hard to justify their teacher's confidence in them. They are proud to be members of Bev's class and want her to continue being proud of them. One word of caution: When you make statements intended to develop pride, make sure they are sincere. Even young children are intuitive enough to see through disingenuous praise.

BE A CONFIDENT GUIDE

As we stated at the beginning of this chapter, two people need to be confident in order to maximize student learning: the student *and* the teacher. The impact of teacher confidence can't be ignored. Many of the students we talked to based their predictions for success on their assessment of teacher confidence. When a teacher is confident in his ability, students have higher expectations for their own learning. Students we talked to affirmed this when describing the confidence of some of their teachers:

"She really knows her stuff, and she explains it so that I can understand."

"My teacher is really good, and he knows how to help me. So I know I can learn it."

Teacher confidence also plays a critical role in classroom management. Confidence leads to clear command of the classroom, which allows students to feel secure. But confidence does not mean complete control. In fact, the only person in your classroom you really have control over is you. Remember, students are ultimately volunteers, and the last thing you need is a coup. Giving some choice and decision making to the students reduces the likelihood of a power struggle and positively impacts class pride. Instead of telling students what *they* are going to do, tell them what *you* are going to do. For example, "I'll talk with you when you lower your voice," or "I'll come assist you when you are seated." These statements allow you to manage your classroom confidently, while ultimately teaching self-discipline to your students—one of the most important non-academic lessons students need to learn. When you help students feel seen and appreciated while holding them to high standards, they will rise to meet your expectations. Be confident in your ability to meet their needs.

Educators grow in confidence the same way students do—by experiencing success. Set a challenging goal for yourself and find a way to monitor your progress. Enlist a colleague who can give you specific performance feedback. Then celebrate small victories on the road to reaching your goal. After all, teachers also enjoy a happy gram, a glitter pencil, or an afternoon in the rolling chair.

Our friend and first grade teacher, Holly, set a goal for increasing her effectiveness with struggling readers. She aspired to become certified in a multi-sensory method of teaching reading, a three-year process. For those three years, she completed courses, observed others, practiced, and sought feedback. She not only saw big gains in the reading achievement levels of her students, but she also experienced a big confidence boost in her own instructional effectiveness.

We love a sign Toni, a school secretary, hung on her office wall that reads, "My track record for getting through tough days is 100 percent." We all need this reminder that our past successes are evidence of our competence, and our past successes are great reasons to be confident. So be sure to make room for achievements on your map. Surround yourself with people who believe in you, so you can borrow their confidence in you when your own is lacking. Most importantly, pay attention to your own self-talk. If you are telling yourself things leading you to doubt your ability, replace those messages. Resist the urge to compare yourself to others and focus on your own progress instead. By growing in competence, you will grow in confidence. And when you are more confident, you perform better. The confidence-competence connection has big implications for your map.

Map-Changing Actions

Since confidence is built on accomplishments, recognizing and remembering your achievements is key to greater confidence. But it can be uncomfortable to brag about yourself or talk about the things that make you proud. One strategy is to create an accomplishment box. Find a shoebox or other small box and fill it with reminders of your successes. If you have pictures, medals, or newspaper articles, put them in the box. If there is no tangible reminder, jot down a note about the accomplishment and put it in the box. Periodically, revisit the box—especially when you need a confidence boost.

Map-Changing Questions

1. How will you help your students grow in both competence and confidence?

2. How will you help your students recognize, celebrate, and remember their achievements?

3. What past successes can you call upon when you need to feel confident?

4. How does your own level of confidence impact those you teach and lead?

SHARE YOUR JOURNEY WITH OTHER MAP CHANGERS USING THE #UNMAPPEDED HASHTAG.

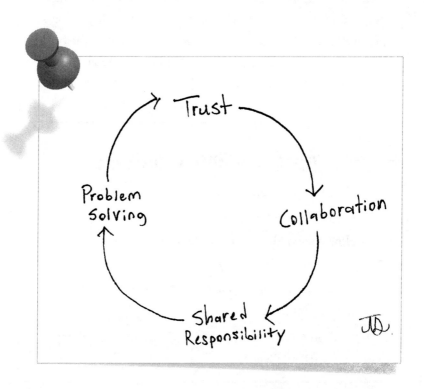

Collaboration is the Key

AMONG ALL THE SIGNIFICANT CULTURAL CON-TRIBUTIONS FROM THE 80S AND 90S, ONE LIKELY STANDS ABOVE THE REST: THE BOY BAND. Few could dispute the impact of Boyz II Men, Backstreet Boys, New Kids on the Block, or *NSYNC. The appeal of these groups lies in their diversity and ability to collaborate. Boy bands are comprised of a cast of characters: the bad boy, the fashion forward guy, the clean cut All-American, and the baby of the group. Diverse personas and complementary vocal abilities make the group look and sound more interesting. Boy band members rarely have the same kind of success as solo artists as they had with the group. The harmony and partner-ship of the boy band draws their fans. In the same way, diverse teams working collaboratively can make a powerful impact on your school.

Perhaps you work in a congenial environment where people are helpful and friendly, talking about weekend activities and Monday Night Football. Even better, maybe you work in an environment where people are collegial, talking about student needs and professional practice. They share resources and model strategies at faculty meetings. While this is good, it is not enough. The complex challenges existing in schools today require us to move beyond collegiality to collaboration. Collaboration requires shared ownership of problems and interactive problem-solving. A truly collaborative team does more than meet occasionally to discuss T-shirt sales or the next field trip. Effective teams do the heavy lifting in successful schools. These teams create schedules, revise discipline plans and address school culture issues. No single educator brings the knowledge, skills, and energy to this work the way a collective group of committed educators does. None of us is as smart as *all* of us.

SHARING THE RIDE

Putting educators on a team or forming a committee is not a complete solution to any problem. Teams are a vehicle to reach an outcome—a means to an end rather than an end in itself. The outcome, or common purpose, is the driving force. But throwing people together and hoping they will work productively is ineffective. Collaborative teams are not just formed; they are built over time in the context of their work. The work of collaboration requires a great deal of time and commitment as teams continuously plan, take action, and reflect on their impact. Collaboration cannot be mandated; it is ultimately a voluntary process. Team members must believe collaboration allows them to achieve bigger outcomes than they can accomplish individually. They must also believe in the benefits of diverse skill sets and perspectives. These beliefs, plus commitment to the common purpose, are essential characteristics of team members. When it comes to building teams, commitment and willingness always trump knowledge and skill.

Because true collaboration is a voluntary process, members must see it as a way to satisfy their own needs and goals. Merging individual aims into a common purpose is critical because the power of a team lies in working toward a common goal. Therefore, the purpose must be clear, compelling, urgent, and attainable. In other words, the purpose of collaboration must be understood by everyone and important enough to justify the time and effort needed to achieve it. The purpose must have an urgency driving team members to act without delaying. In schools, the common purpose typically revolves around maximizing student learning, boosting student achievement, or eliminating an achievement gap. Allowing team members time to buy into the purpose before jumping into an action plan is crucial for long-term results.

THE TRAIL MIX

The two of us recently observed a team of educators collaborating on an intervention plan for their school. The team consisted of one teacher from each subject area, a teacher of students with disabilities, and a guidance counselor. Each team member brought a unique and important perspective to the work. If the team consisted of only guidance counselors, the challenges identified by the subject area teachers would have been overlooked. If the team was made up only of teachers, they would have lacked the schoolwide scheduling expertise of the guidance counselor. Instead, the diversity of perspectives ensured a comprehensive intervention plan.

Teams thrive when people with diverse and complementary strengths come together. Teams of like thinkers are less effective because like-minded people often reach the similar conclusions.

Because each of our individual perspectives is limited, multiple perspectives are much more comprehensive. A variety of perspectives, skills and strengths make up a dynamic team. After all, it takes more than just peanuts to make a good trail mix.

IT TAKES MORE THAN
JUST PEANUTS TO MAKE
A GOOD TRAIL MIX.

In addition to diversity, four characteristics are common to high-performing teams: clear roles, efficient communication, productive processes, and effective leadership. Clear roles maximize the benefits of diversity. Therefore, a team should base roles on each individual's strengths and skills. Clarity of roles happens with plenty of discussion so each member understands all members' functions. Ongoing discussion also ensures equitable division of tasks. Fairly and equitably distributing the work prevents members from burning out or becoming resentful. Clear roles are especially important when interdependence is required to reach a goal.

Ants are nature's ultimate collaborators. Individually, they are limited, but together they create amazing living structures and find food for the whole colony. Ants have specific roles but are committed to a collective purpose. In the ant colony, there are queens, drones, and workers. The survival of the colony depends on the ants performing their roles as part of the collective goals of building, feeding, and reproducing. In the same way, collaborative team members depend on one another to achieve their goals.

Interdependence occurs when each member's actions influence the performance of other members. When you must work interactively in order to succeed, interdependence is essential. It requires a high degree of trust and a high level of commitment to a common purpose. Two seniors from our local high school have recently embarked on an interdependent business venture. One has passion and skill as a web designer; the other is a talented web developer. One can make beautiful websites, but they don't always function optimally. The other can make functional websites, but they aren't particularly pretty. Together, though, they create fabulous websites for their classmates and clients. Likewise, when teams of educators work together, the outcome reflects their collective strengths.

Efficient communication and productive processes are hallmarks of high-performing teams. We live just a few hours from the Daytona International Speedway. Watching the pit crews at the racetrack gives us a prime example of communication and clearly defined processes. Pit crews communicate in a fast, clear, and direct way. They are intentional and focused on the task at hand because there is no time to waste on misunderstanding or confusion. The processes of these pit crews, like the processes of all high-performing teams, fall into two types: implementation and deliberation. Implementation processes focus on the work. At Daytona, this might be changing a tire; at our school, this could be analyzing student work samples. Deliberation processes focus on thinking, such as brainstorming, problem-solving, or reflecting. A diverse team, with a variety of skills and perspectives, has a powerful collective intelligence, but it will only be effective if communication and processes are clear and efficient.

Teams cannot be high performing without effective leadership. Leaders communicate the common purpose and guide the team toward achieving it. They facilitate the discussions through which teams develop roles and procedures. Great leaders view their roles as a service to the team, and they know and appreciate the diverse strengths of the individual members as well as the collective capacity of the team. Most importantly, effective leaders have unwavering belief in the potential of their team and unwavering commitment to the collective purpose. These leaders promote the positive climate, helping team members cope with setbacks and persevere through challenges. Collaboration cannot be mandated, and neither can leadership. Effective leaders are not just appointed; they are intentionally developed over time.

Teacher leader, Mandy, leads a team of fifth-grade teachers at a high-needs elementary school. Mandy keeps the team focused on their purpose: to plan celebrations for their students and prepare them for entering middle school. Mandy has delegated tasks with team members' strengths in mind. She knows that one member can effectively communicate with the middle school, facilitating the students' transition. She knows that another team member possesses the detailed focus needed to plan a big party, culminating the years of growth and achievement students experienced in elementary school. Although the team experiences challenges throughout the year, Mandy's positive outlook keeps the team on track. Mandy often has reflective conversations with her principal and asks her team for feedback in an effort to continually grow and develop as a leader.

BUILDING TRUST

Building trust is a necessary first step in creating a truly collaborative school culture. While we might find it easier to trust those who are like us in terms of race, age, gender, or background, diversity is necessary for true collaboration; we must build trust across our differences. Schools growing and sustaining productive teams are characterized by strong trusting relationships. If we believe collaboration is necessary to solve schoolwide problems, we must seek to grow schoolwide trust. The trust-collaboration loop is undeniable. The more we collaborate, the more opportunities we have to build trust. And the more we trust one another, the more likely we are to collaborate.

All relationships have some degree of emotional risk, and risk necessitates trust. But you cannot trust others without first trusting yourself. With the potential for disappointment, you must trust yourself to deal with the impact of someone letting you down. In order to extend trust, you must believe you will ultimately be okay, even if your trust is not well placed. For example, we will trust a colleague to complete a critical part of a group task only if we believe we can handle the outcome if she does not follow through.

Several ingredients are needed to develop trust. The first is benevolence, the belief the other person will act in your best interest. In other words, you must believe the other person "has your back" in order for you to trust him. One way to show benevolence is to disclose your rationale for decisions. Since we tend to make assumptions about others' intentions, others will make assumptions about ours if we don't fill in the blanks for them. Our colleague, Sam, became the principal of a struggling school, and he decided he would walk through classrooms after school each day to give teachers an opportunity to talk and share their concerns with him. However, because he didn't share his reason for the after school walk-throughs, teachers assumed he was checking to see if they were working, and Sam had to do some backpedaling to prove his benevolent intentions and restore trust.

Reliability is the second ingredient needed to develop trust. Reliability is more than just showing up; it is following through and delivering what you promised. In order to be reliable, you must be organized and even-tempered. Forgetting obligations and canceling appointments leads others to question your reliability.

The third trust ingredient is competence, which encompasses having the ability to perform a needed task and an accurate assessment of your skills related to that task. People tend to trust us if they believe we are capable of doing something, know what we are talking about, and can admit when we don't. That means that part of being competent is knowing when and how to ask for help.

Honesty and transparency are the final ingredients of trust. Representing situations truthfully and fairly is crucial for building trust. People may not always want to hear the truth, but they appreciate honesty. You do not need to be brutally honest—just tell the truth. Like honesty, transparency requires freely sharing information. When we are transparent, we disclose our intentions, and we don't hide the good, the bad, or the ugly.

These trust ingredients indicate we have to know someone (at least a little bit) before we can trust him. Teachers sometimes scoff at the teambuilding activities in faculty meetings. But the back-to-school bingo game is an important step in building trusting relationships—so embrace it. Earlier in our careers, we opened a new school together, drawing faculty from across the district. The first thing we did was send our new staff on a scavenger hunt. We knew while they were interacting, team members would begin getting to know one another, which would eventually evolve into trusting one another.

When teachers trust one another and collaborate, they ultimately have a greater positive impact on students than could have been realized by teachers working independently. Collaboration enhances problem-solving when a diversity of solutions proposed. If you work on a team with like-minded people, you are apt to come up with the same solution you would have found on your own. In contrast, purposefully working with people who have different viewpoints and skills strengthens the team. True teamwork is an active, inclusive, and participatory process. Collaboration turns our individual powers into super powers.

A COMMON PATH

Just as with individual performance, confidence impacts team performance. Collective confidence is an essential element for team success. Our favorite coach, Tony, asserts collective confidence is the most powerful predictor of winning or losing. In other words, winning teams are ones who believe they will win. The modeling of confidence— through either words or actions by one member—can positively impact the other members and, therefore, increase collective confidence. Teams develop self-talk just as individuals do. And when they meet an obstacle, confident teams fully believe in their collective ability to reach a goal. How do you contribute to the collective confidence of your team?

Effective collaboration and successful team performance require the merging of individual goals into a common goal. However, there are both individual and collective benefits. When you collaborate with others, you broaden your own perspectives, increase your own capacity, and extend beyond your comfort zone. Each map has its own inherent limitations. When we put our maps together, we are collectively wiser. With multiple maps at the table, we see a more accurate view of the problem and generate a more comprehensive solution. Collaboration takes time and commitment, but it is key for lasting schoolwide change.

Map-Changing Actions

Collaborating is about knowing and tapping into others' strengths when you need answers and assistance. It is built on knowing your colleagues and trusting their character and competence. Take note of who does what well at your school. Look beyond the boundaries of grade level, subject area, role, or age. Pay particular attention to people who complement, rather than match, your strengths. Create a map of "colleague capital," a simple table showing your colleagues' or team members' unique strengths, skills, or knowledge. Once completed, take a step back and admire the collective brilliance in your school and use it as a resource when collaboration is needed.

Map-Changing Questions

1. To what degree do you currently collaborate with colleagues?

2. What could you gain by collaborating more?

3. How could your students benefit from your collaboration?

4. What obstacles get in the way of collaboration at your school?

5. What are you willing to do about those obstacles?

SHARE YOUR JOURNEY
WITH OTHER MAP
CHANGERS USING THE
#UNMAPPEDED HASHTAG.

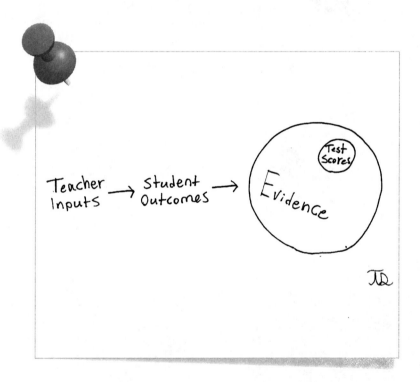

Traveling within the System

IF YOU LOOK CLOSELY, YOU MAY FIND IN YOUR SCHOOLS THE RARE AND WONDERFUL THIRTY-YEAR, VETERAN EDUCATOR WHO IS STILL PUMPED AND PASSIONATE ABOUT TEACHING AND LEARNING. Despite the always challenging and sometimes hazardous environment, these amazing teachers have defied the odds. We encountered one recently at a local high school and convinced him to reveal his secrets. "I've been a teacher for thirty-two years," he said, "and I have never had the same year twice. There are always new things to learn about students, about pedagogy, and about the world." He explained that, at the beginning of each school year, he seeks out the new teachers. "I like to partner up with the ones straight out of college. They think I am mentoring them, but they are mentoring me. These kids know the latest tech tools and the latest terminology." He keeps his focus on the bigger purpose: helping his students learn and grow. He saves his energy for the important items, rather than fretting over small stuff. "You always have to remember why you started," he shared, "and I became a teacher to make a difference." Keeping your focus on your *why* is a resiliency booster for all educators, whether in year three or year thirty-three.

The students in this veteran's class obviously adored him. As we talked to them, their comments revealed his unique characteristics. Authenticity was a big factor in his success, and he had a deep understanding of his beliefs, values, and the greater purpose for his work. His instructional choices and actions aligned with the vision he created of the educator he wanted to be. He had his own way of teaching and relating to students, and they responded positively to it. He had rejected practices inconsistent with his style and adapted others to fit his own beliefs, values, and purpose.

CHOOSING YOUR ROUTE

As principals, we are committed to coaching and growing teachers, and we have worked with a number of struggling teachers. As we thought about this veteran teacher, we had an epiphany: teachers who appear to lack skill may actually simply lack clarity. They may not yet have clarified their own philosophy or teaching style. One teacher we worked with struggled to elicit the same level of student achievement as the other teachers on her third grade team. She was intelligent and hardworking, and she willingly tried the strategies we suggested, so her lack of success didn't make sense. During an observation in her class one day, the underlying problem suddenly became clear. She had been advised to incorporate more student discussion into her lessons because her students did not seem to be consistently engaged.

At several points in the lesson, she asked students to turn and talk to one another, but it didn't seem to work for her. She was incorporating discussion because she knew she was supposed to, but she didn't understand why. She didn't know we give students opportunities to talk because we value student voice, because we believe learning is an active process, and because we believe knowledge is socially constructed. She didn't really have a compelling reason for using student discussion, and she didn't have enough clarity about her own values and beliefs to decide whether this strategy fit her style.

When you understand the philosophy and beliefs behind a resource or strategy and you know what you believe about teaching and learning, you can ensure authenticity. In other words, never do anything just because everybody else is doing it. While many pedagogical techniques have been shown to correlate with greater learning, they don't all work for all teachers and all students. And effective educators who adopt a new strategy likely will tweak it a bit to better fit their own style. Great teachers have many different teaching styles, but they are always authentic. Be bold and innovative—but always be *you*. You are smart, you are a critical thinker, and this is not your first rodeo. So try new things, but do so with a big fat compelling *why*.

BE BOLD AND
INNOVATIVE—BUT
ALWAYS BE YOU.

Our epiphany also revealed a lesson for anyone with influence over educational policy. Instead of reform initiatives focused on specific programs, why not focus on developing educators' capacity for critical thinking, problem-solving, and persevering? Why not invest in people over programs? After all, laying any new program, product, or strategy on top of limiting beliefs is like building on a faulty foundation. Starting with beliefs and expectations ensures each educator has a strong foundation to build on.

EMPOWERING ALL TRAVELERS

Truthfully, though, any change impacting educators has a low probability of succeeding without their input in the planning and implementation. Just like students, educators need choice and voice. An endless imposition of mandates, scripted curriculum, and lock-step pacing guides communicates little belief in teacher competence, and an overprescribed curriculum limits teachers' capacity for growth. Since the inverse relationship between belief in ability and need for control impacts educators just as it does students, we could better support them in their growth as teachers if we invested in their development, listened to their opinions, and involved them in decision making. As they grow in their abilities, we are able to believe in them more. And the more we believe in someone's ability, the less we need to control.

Through the ups and downs in our combined fifty years in education, we have learned one thing for sure: if lasting reform is to take hold in a school, it will come from within. The best solutions come from a familiarity with the unique context of a school and an intimate knowledge of its purpose. Teaching and learning is complex and dynamic; we cannot fully capture its overall effectiveness with a single score on an annual test. Unfortunately, the availability and efficiency of test scores make them very attractive. Scores, however, are only a small representation of a bigger story. They ignore the human characteristics and unique circumstances of students; and an overreliance on test scores leads to systematized, standardized, and homogenized practices (think George Orwell's *1984*). We are not in the manufacturing business; we are in the business of helping people grow.

So where does data fit into school reform? We heard one superintendent say data is a "great servant and an awful master." In other words, we should allow data to inform us but not drive us. It is a useful tool but never an end in itself. Data only tells us where we are right now and has absolutely no bearing on where we end up. However, data can be empowering when used correctly. When we use data to accurately assess where we are, and we know where we want to go, we can use the data to make a plan for getting there. Additionally, using it to track progress over time can be motivating. Let's keep in mind that test scores are one tiny piece of a bigger picture. Evidence of student learning encompasses so much more.

APPRECIATING DIFFERENT PERSPECTIVES

If we are to transform our schools successfully, we have to work together. We cannot be *us* and *them*. If we all have the same goal—to better reach and teach all students—there is only *us*. At the school level, teachers and administrators may appear to be on different teams, and it can be difficult for each to understand the other's perspective. Even though most principals were once teachers, the extensive demands of their administrative roles make it difficult for them to remember what it was like to be in the classroom. The longer we are out of the classroom, the murkier those memories become. Teachers may also have some misconceptions about leading a school. Actually, the authority principals have over students, parents, staff members, and circumstances is often overestimated. Viewing principals as having unlimited power can make them seem invulnerable. The truth is that both teachers and principals are human; we all have our ups and downs.

Due to misperceptions about their power and control, principals often shoulder the blame for any source of dissatisfaction or frustration in the school. Granted, some problems really are our fault but not all of them. Similarly, because teachers have direct contact with students, they may shoulder the blame for student issues. Since the reality is both teachers and principals have limited power and neither has a complete picture without the other, working together is imperative. If principals can find ways to protect teachers from unnecessary burdens and distractions, and teachers can find ways to take ownership of some schoolwide issues, we create a powerful partnership. When school reform is imperative, somebody needs to do something; and that somebody is us.

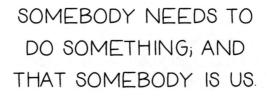

SOMEBODY NEEDS TO DO SOMETHING; AND THAT SOMEBODY IS US.

Our friend, Alan, is a middle school social studies teacher at a school adjusting to a recent change of principal. The former principal was autocratic, with a high need for control. She carefully looked at data and made decisions—by herself. Sometimes her decisions didn't make sense to the teachers because she never considered their perspective, which was very frustrating for the faculty. But there was one undeniable benefit: as long as they weren't involved in the decision making, they had a free pass to complain. If they didn't have a say, they didn't have any ownership of the consequences.

When the new principal arrived, she involved teachers in making key decisions for the school, but to her surprise, some teachers did not want to have voice or choice. Sitting back and complaining about decisions was easier for them. However, over time, the faculty began to see including diverse perspectives ultimately resulted in better decisions for their students and their school, and sharing ownership of school decisions created a more impactful and coherent faculty.

The notion of teacher leadership hardly seems radical. Anyone who can get twenty kindergarteners to walk in a straight line obviously possesses leadership ability. Teachers bring an important perspective, and their unique skills and knowledge are useful in identifying and solving schoolwide problems. Teachers are also in a key position to influence their colleagues. Sometimes the success of a change depends on who is supporting it, and teachers can provide firsthand knowledge about how well something works. When influential teachers model commitment to a proposed solution, others are likely to follow their lead. Smart principals know and leverage the strengths of their teachers as a way to share leadership responsibilities in their schools. However, principals must avoid the temptation to keep piling responsibilities on the tried and true performers. We have to spread the opportunities—potential stars are waiting for a chance to shine.

STOPPING FOR GAS

Educator burnout is one of the biggest obstacles to lasting school reform. Subtle pressure exists for us to work long hours and continuously do more to prove our commitment to students. We work in a field where sacrifice is valued and admired. Bragging rights come with having the first or the last car in the parking lot. We don't even try to conceal the dark under-eye circles we developed during late-night planning or grading sessions. Unfortunately, the possibility for more work is endless; there is always something more to take on. Instead of adding more, we need to prioritize our own learning and growth, as well as our health and well-being. Transformation and growth is far more inspirational than sacrifice and strain. We don't need martyrs; we need missionaries. We need educators on a mission to uncover the limitless potential in all students.

WE DON'T NEED MARTYRS;
WE NEED MISSIONARIES.
WE NEED EDUCATORS ON
A MISSION TO UNCOVER
THE LIMITLESS POTENTIAL
IN ALL STUDENTS.

Resilient teachers gain energy through networking with colleagues inside and outside of their schools. They share both professional resources and emotional support. They encourage one another to find a balance between their work and personal lives. In a bubble of connection, we find strength in numbers and power to withstand a host of outside pressures. What are you doing to keep your passion burning instead of burning out?

While we can't continue to do more things, we *can* do things differently. Continuously implementing new programs is not the path to lasting change. We can only build lasting change on a foundation of empowering beliefs and expectations. First, believe in the unlimited potential of your students, your colleagues, and yourself. Cultivate your own competence and confidence. Then carefully choose what meets your needs and fits the unique context of your school. Educators are professionals with the creativity and wisdom to bring about change, but we may first need to make some adjustments to our maps.

Map-Changing Actions

If you are harboring limiting beliefs about your school, your district, or even your profession, replace them. Teachers know giving up a teaching resource or strategy without something new to replace it is difficult. Likewise, getting rid of an existing belief without a new belief to take its place is also challenging. When you identify a limiting belief, create an empowering belief to replace it. For example, believing *nobody appreciates me* is limiting. However, believing *those I teach and lead benefit from my hard work* is empowering. Write your new belief at the top of a note card. As you go through your day, look for evidence to confirm the new belief and write that evidence on the card, too. Do this until the new belief becomes stronger than the old one.

Map-Changing Questions

1. What are your core beliefs about teaching and learning?

2. How do the practices and the strategies you use align with those core beliefs?

3. What would your students say makes you "uniquely you" as a teacher or leader?

4. How can you remain a purposeful and passionate teacher or leader over time?

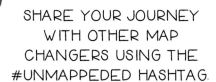

SHARE YOUR JOURNEY
WITH OTHER MAP
CHANGERS USING THE
#UNMAPPEDED HASHTAG.

Perfection

A•————•B

Reality

A

JD

You Never Really Get There

10

WE LOVE THE DIY NETWORK. DIY features nonstop shows about how to "do it yourself"—remodel your bathroom, build a raised garden bed, make new things out of old barn wood, and even flip a house. Like the projects featured on DIY, changing your map is definitely a do-it-yourself job. However, this task doesn't wrap up neatly in a thirty-minute show. Changing your limiting beliefs and purposefully becoming the educator you envision is not a one-and-done event. Unlike earning a college degree you acquire once and keep forever, changing your map is a continuous process of cultivating awareness, making conscious choices, and evaluating outcomes. Simply watching a TV show doesn't result in an updated kitchen; simply reading this book is unlikely to result in any lasting change. Information alone never leads to transformation; you must take action. Hold yourself accountable and commit to doing the work.

Progress, however, doesn't happen in a neat, linear way. We don't go straight from point A to point B. At times, we take one step forward and two steps back. So give yourself a break when you go off course. Challenges and obstacles are always on the road to lasting change, and mistakes are evidence you are trying something new. Feeling happy and satisfied when things are going well is easy, but staying positive when difficulties and setbacks come around is more challenging. Sometimes, difficulties arise as the result of your choices; other times, they are a result of things beyond your control. Remember ... you may not be able to prevent a problem, but you can always choose your response.

DON'T TAKE THE JOURNEY ALONE

Our best advice for getting through the rough terrain is to find a travel companion. A fellow map changer will encourage you to keep going when you feel like giving up. A great co-pilot will loan you some confidence when yours is running low. Most importantly, a true travel companion can give you honest feedback and help you reflect because, sometimes, others see us more clearly than we see ourselves. The two of us have found many gifts like these in our own professional partnership. We are undoubtedly stronger and braver together than either of us would be on our own. Individually, we have different strengths and dispositions, but our diversity is key to our collaboration. You may have to pick up a few passengers before you find the right travel companion, but once you find yours, buckle up and don't look back.

There are many reasons for embarking on this map-changing journey, but perhaps the best reason is you cannot expect your students to go where you are not willing to go. You can't expect students to believe in their limitless potential if you hold limiting beliefs about your own.

You can't expect students to do what it takes to grow in competence and confidence when you aren't doing the work personally. You can't expect students to take risks and embrace mistakes if you don't. You can't expect students to be engaged and passionate if you are worn out and weary. After all, you weren't meant to live a perfect life; you were meant to live a purposeful life.

> YOU WEREN'T MEANT TO LIVE A PERFECT LIFE; YOU WERE MEANT TO LIVE A PURPOSEFUL LIFE.

One of the best parts of our work is the "do over" each year as summer turns to fall. At the beginning of summer, we reflect and bring closure to the previous year. As we turn to fall, we see the opportunity to make different choices and celebrate a new beginning. We have the choice to start each year with positive expectations. Last year is the past; today is a new beginning.

Create a powerful vision of the educator you want to be. Assess where you are compared to your vision. Does your current map hold beliefs and patterns to help you reach your goal? If not, your map is not serving you well. Every map eventually becomes outdated and needs revision from time to time. Revise your map and plan a route to get from where you are to where you want to be. Don't worry if you go off course—just make a U-turn and get back on track. Take bold steps in the direction of your dreams. And know we will be cheering you on!

Map-Changing Actions

Upon waking each morning, say to yourself, "This is a new day." Spend a few moments thinking about how you would like to live this day. Then set an intention for your day. For example: "Today I will be more compassionate with myself and others." Carry this intention with you and let it influence your thoughts and actions throughout the day. In this way, you will purposefully create your day, rather than letting circumstances and others determine how your day unfolds.

Map-Changing Questions

1. What is your vision for the educator you would like to be?

2. How is your vision different from where you are right now?

3. What do you need to do to get from here to there?

4. What will you gain by reaching your goal?

5. Who can you identify as a fellow map changer and travel companion?

SHARE YOUR JOURNEY
WITH OTHER MAP
CHANGERS USING THE
#UNMAPPEDED HASHTAG

Acknowledgments

We would like to express our sincere gratitude to Dave and Shelley Burgess, and the entire Dave Burgess Consulting, Inc. team, for bringing this book to life.

Resources

Anderson, E. Strengths-Based Educating: A Concrete Way to Bring Out the Best in Students—and Yourself. *Educational Horizons*, 2005. Vol. 8 No. 3, 180-189.

Bandura, A. Self-Efficacy. *Encyclopedia of Health and Behavior*. Thousand Oaks, CA: Sage, 2004.

Beaudoin, M. & Taylor, M. *Creating a Positive School Culture: How Principals and Teachers Can Solve Problems Together*. Thousand Oaks, CA: Corwin Press, 2004.

Berdik, C. *Mind Over Mind: The Surprising Power of Expectations*. New York, NY: Current, 2012.

Briceño, E. Mistakes are not all created equal. *Mindset Works*. January 10, 2015. Retrieved from: blog.mindsetworks.com/blog-page/home-blogs/entry/mistakes-are-not-all-created-equal.

Burgess, D. *Teach Like a Pirate: Increase Student Engagement, Boost Your Creativity, and Transform Your Life as an Educator*. San Diego, CA: Dave Burgess Consulting, Inc., 2012.

Dufour, R. & Marzano, R. *Leaders of Learning: How District, School, and Classroom Leaders Improve Student Achievement*. Bloomington, IN: Solution Tree Press, 2011.

Dweck, C. *Mindset: A New Psychology of Success*. New York, NY: Random House, 2008.

Fullan, M. *Change Leader: Learning to Do what Matters Most*. San Francisco, CA: Jossey-Bass, 2011.

Hassler, C. *Expectation Hangover: Overcoming Disappointment in Work, Love, and Life*. Novato, CA: New World Library, 2014.

Hoobyar, T. & Dotz, T. *The Essential Guide to Neuro-Linguistic Programming*. New York, NY: Harper Collins, 2013.

Houston, P. & Sokolow, S. *The Spiritual Dimension of Leadership: 8 Key Principles to Leading More Effectively*. Thousand Oaks, CA: Corwin Press, 2006.

Jackson, Y. *The Pedagogy of Confidence: Inspiring High Intellectual Performance in Urban Schools*. New York, NY: Teachers College Press, 2011.

Rosenthal, R. & Jacobson, L. *Pygmalion in the Classroom: Teacher Expectation and Pupils' Intellectual Development*. Bethel, CT: Crown House Publishing LTD, 1992.

Rubin, G. *Better than Before: What I Learned About Making And Breaking Habits—To Sleep More, Quit Sugar, Procrastinate Less, And Generally Build A Happy Life*. New York, NY: Broadway Books, 2015.

Seligman, Martin. *Learned Optimism: How to Change Your Mind and Your Life*. New York, NY: Vintage Books, 2006.

Smith, P.A., Hoy, W.K., and Sweetland, S.R. Organizational Health of High Schools and Dimensions of Faculty Trust. *Journal of School Leadership 11, no. 2 (March 2001): 135-151*.

Taylor, J. *My Stroke of Insight: A Brain Surgeon's Personal Journey*. New York, NY: Viking, 2006.

Weinstein, R. *Reaching Higher: The Power of Expectations In Schooling*. Cambridge, MA: Harvard University Press, 2002.

Discover Unmapped Potential at Your School

Julie and Missy offer high-impact keynote presentations, seminars, and workshops. Connect with them to see what one principal, one professor, and a whole lot of purpose can do for your school or organization.

MOST REQUESTED TOPICS:

Change Your Map—Change Your School
Charting a Course from Where You Are to Where You Want to Be

Your beliefs and expectations form a mental map that guides your decisions, actions, and relationships. So if you want to take your classroom or school in a new direction, you must start by examining and revising your map. During this interactive journey, you will discover strategies and concrete tools that will transform your teaching and leading. Julie and Missy will equip and empower you so that you can empower students.

Map Changers
Stories of Women Who Lead

Women often carry limiting beliefs on their mental maps. These beliefs impact our decisions, actions, and relationships. During this interactive journey, you will discover strategies and concrete tools that will help you transform limiting beliefs into empowering beliefs. Julie and Missy will share their own leadership stories and the inspirational stories of other women in leadership.

More From Dave Burgess Consulting, Inc.

Teach Like a PIRATE

Increase Student Engagement, Boost Your Creativity, and Transform Your Life as an Educator
By Dave Burgess (@BurgessDave)

   Teach Like a PIRATE is the New York Times' best-selling book that has sparked a worldwide educational revolution. It is part inspirational manifesto that ignites passion for the profession and part practical road map, filled with dynamic strategies to dramatically increase student engagement. Translated into multiple languages, its message resonates with educators who want to design outrageously creative lessons and transform school into a life-changing experience for students.

Learn Like a PIRATE

Empower Your Students to Collaborate, Lead, and Succeed

By Paul Solarz (@PaulSolarz)

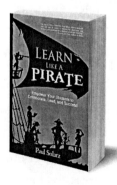

   Today's job market demands that students be prepared to take responsibility for their lives and careers. We do them a disservice if we teach them how to earn passing grades without equipping them to take charge of their education. In *Learn Like a PIRATE*, Paul Solarz explains how to design classroom experiences that encourage students to take risks and explore their passions in a stimulating, motivating, and supportive environment where improvement, rather than grades, is the focus. Discover how student-led classrooms help students thrive and develop into self-directed, confident citizens who are capable of making smart, responsible decisions, all on their own.

P is for PIRATE

Inspirational ABC's for Educators

By Dave and Shelley Burgess (@Burgess_Shelley)

Teaching is an adventure that stretches the imagination and calls for creativity every day! In *P is for PIRATE*, husband and wife team Dave and Shelley Burgess encourage and inspire educators to make their classrooms fun and exciting places to learn. Tapping into years of personal experience and drawing on the insights of more than seventy educators, the authors offer a wealth of ideas for making learning and teaching more fulfilling than ever before.

Play Like a Pirate

Engage Students with Toys, Games, and Comics

by Quinn Rollins (@jedikermit)

Yes! School can be simultaneously fun and educational. In *Play Like a Pirate*, Quinn Rollins offers practical, engaging strategies and resources that make it easy to integrate fun into your curriculum. Regardless of the grade level you teach, you'll find inspiration and ideas that will help you engage your students in unforgettable ways.

eXPlore Like a Pirate

Gamification and Game-Inspired Course Design to Engage, Enrich, and Elevate Your Learners

By Michael Matera (@MrMatera)

Are you ready to transform your classroom into an experiential world that flourishes on collaboration and creativity? Then set sail with classroom game designer and educator Michael Matera as he reveals the possibilities and power of game-based learning. In *eXPlore Like a Pirate*, Matera serves as your experienced guide to help you apply the most motivational techniques of gameplay to your classroom. You'll learn gamification strategies that will work with and enhance (rather than replace) your current curriculum and discover how these engaging methods can be applied to any grade level or subject.

Lead Like a PIRATE

Make School Amazing for Your Students and Staff

By Shelley Burgess and Beth Houf
(@Burgess_Shelley, @BethHouf)

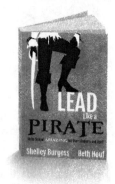

In *Lead Like a PIRATE*, education leaders Shelley Burgess and Beth Houf map out the character traits necessary to captain a school or district. You'll learn where to find the treasure that's already in your classrooms and schools—and how to bring out the very best in your educators. This book will equip and encourage you to be relentless in your quest to make school amazing for your students, staff, parents, and communities.

The Zen Teacher

Creating FOCUS, SIMPLICITY, and TRANQUILITY in the Classroom

By Dan Tricarico (@TheZenTeacher)

Teachers have incredible power to influence—even improve—the future. In *The Zen Teacher*, educator, blogger, and speaker Dan Tricarico provides practical, easy-to-use techniques to help teachers be their best—unrushed and fully focused—so they can maximize their performance and improve their quality of life. In this introductory guide, Dan Tricarico explains what it means to develop a Zen practice—something that has nothing to do with religion and everything to do with your ability to thrive in the classroom.

Master the Media

How Teaching Media Literacy Can Save Our Plugged-in World

By Julie Smith (@julnilsmith)

Written to help teachers and parents educate the next generation, *Master the Media* explains the history, purpose, and messages behind the media. The point isn't to get kids to unplug; it's to help them make informed choices, understand the difference between truth and lies, and discern perception from reality. Critical thinking leads to smarter decisions—and it's why media literacy can save the world.

The Innovator's Mindset

Empower Learning, Unleash Talent,
and Lead a Culture of Creativity

By George Couros (@gcouros)

The traditional system of education requires students to hold their questions and compliantly stick to the scheduled curriculum. But our job as educators is to provide new and better opportunities for our students. It's time to recognize that compliance doesn't foster innovation, encourage critical thinking, or inspire creativity—and those are the skills our students need to succeed. In *The Innovator's Mindset*, George Couros encourages teachers and administrators to empower their learners to wonder, to explore—and to become forward-thinking leaders.

50 Things You Can Do with Google Classroom

By Alice Keeler and Libbi Miller
(@AliceKeeler, @MillerLibbi)

It can be challenging to add new technology to the classroom, but it's a must if students are going to be well-equipped for the future. Alice Keeler and Libbi Miller shorten the learning curve by providing a thorough overview of the Google Classroom App. Part of Google Apps for Education (GAfE), Google Classroom was specifically designed to help teachers save time by streamlining the process of going digital. Complete with screenshots, *50 Things You Can Do with Google Classroom* provides ideas and step-by-step instructions to help teachers implement this powerful tool.

50 Things to Go Further with Google Classroom

A Student-Centered Approach

By Alice Keeler and Libbi Miller
(@AliceKeeler, @MillerLibbi)

Today's technology empowers educators to move away from the traditional classroom where teachers lead and students work independently—each doing the same thing. In *50 Things to Go Further with Google Classroom: A Student-Centered Approach*, authors and educators Alice Keeler and Libbi Miller offer inspiration and resources to help you create a digitally rich, engaging, student-centered environment. They show you how to tap into the power of individualized learning that is possible with Google Classroom.

Pure Genius

*Building a Culture of Innovation and
Taking 20% Time to the Next Level*

By Don Wettrick (@DonWettrick)

For far too long, schools have been bastions of boredom, killers of creativity, and way too comfortable with compliance and conformity. In *Pure Genius*, Don Wettrick explains how collaboration—with experts, students, and other educators—can help you create interesting, and even life-changing, opportunities for learning. Wettrick's book inspires and equips educators with a systematic blueprint for teaching innovation in any school.

140 Twitter Tips for Educators

*Get Connected, Grow Your Professional
Learning Network, and Reinvigorate Your Career*

By Brad Currie, Billy Krakower, and Scott Rocco
(@bradmcurrie, @wkrakower, @ScottRRocco)

Whatever questions you have about education or about how you can be even better at your job, you'll find ideas, resources, and a vibrant network of professionals ready to help you on Twitter. In *140 Twitter Tips for Educators*, #Satchat hosts and founders of Evolving Educators, Brad Currie, Billy Krakower, and Scott Rocco, offer step-by-step instructions to help you master the basics of Twitter, build an online following, and become a Twitter rock star.

Ditch That Textbook

*Free Your Teaching and Revolutionize
Your Classroom*

By Matt Miller (@jmattmiller)

Textbooks are symbols of centuries-old education. They're often outdated as soon as they hit students' desks. Acting "by the textbook" implies compliance and a lack of creativity. It's time to ditch those textbooks—and those textbook assumptions about learning! In *Ditch That Textbook*, teacher and blogger Matt Miller encourages educators to throw out meaningless, pedestrian teaching and learning practices. He empowers them to evolve and improve on old, standard teaching methods. *Ditch That Textbook* is a support system, toolbox, and manifesto to help educators free their teaching and revolutionize their classrooms.

How Much Water Do We Have?

5 Success Principles for Conquering Any
Change and Thriving in Times of Change

by Pete Nunweiler with Kris Nunweiler

In *How Much Water Do We Have?* Pete Nunweiler identifies five key elements—information, planning, motivation, support, and leadership—that are necessary for the success of any goal, life transition, or challenge. Referring to these elements as the 5 Waters of Success, Pete explains that, like the water we drink, you need them to thrive in today's rapidly paced world. If you're feeling stressed out, overwhelmed, or uncertain at work or at home, pause and look for the signs of dehydration. Learn how to find, acquire, and use the 5 Waters of Success—so you can share them with your team and family members.

Instant Relevance

Using Today's Experiences
in Tomorrow's Lessons

By Denis Sheeran (@MathDenisNJ)

Every day, students in schools around the world ask the question, "When am I ever going to use this in real life?" In *Instant Relevance*, author and keynote speaker Denis Sheeran equips you to create engaging lessons *from* experiences and events that matter to your students. Learn how to help your students see meaningful connections between the real world and what they learn in the classroom—because that's when learning sticks.

The Classroom Chef

Sharpen Your Lessons. Season Your Classes.
Make Math Meaningful.

By John Stevens and Matt Vaudrey
(@Jstevens009, @MrVaudrey)

In *The Classroom Chef*, math teachers and instructional coaches John Stevens and Matt Vaudrey share their secret recipes, ingredients, and tips for serving up lessons that engage students and help them "get" math. You can use these ideas and methods as-is, or better yet, tweak them and create your own enticing educational meals. The message the authors share is that, with imagination and preparation, every teacher can be a Classroom Chef.

Start. Right. Now.

Teach and Lead for Excellence

By Todd Whitaker, Jeff Zoul, and Jimmy Casas
(@ToddWhitaker, @Jeff_Zoul, @casas_jimmy)

In their work leading up to *Start. Right. Now.*, Todd Whitaker, Jeff Zoul, and Jimmy Casas studied educators from across the nation and discovered four key behaviors of excellence: Excellent leaders and teachers *Know the Way, Show the Way, Go the Way, and Grow Each Day*. If you are ready to take the first step toward excellence, this motivating book will put you on the right path.

The Writing on the Classroom Wall

How Posting Your Most Passionate Beliefs about Education Can Empower Your Students, Propel Your Growth, and Lead to a Lifetime of Learning

By Steve Wyborney (@SteveWyborney)

In *The Writing on the Classroom Wall*, Steve Wyborney explains how posting and discussing Big Ideas can lead to deeper learning. You'll learn why sharing your ideas will sharpen and refine them. You'll also be encouraged to know that the Big Ideas you share don't have to be profound to make a profound impact on learning. In fact, Steve explains, it's okay if some of your ideas fall *off* the wall. What matters most is sharing them.

LAUNCH

Using Design Thinking to Boost Creativity and Bring Out the Maker in Every Student

By John Spencer and A.J. Juliani
(@spencerideas, @ajjuliani)

Something happens in students when they define themselves as *makers* and *inventors* and *creators*. They discover powerful skills—problem-solving, critical thinking, and imagination—that will help them shape the world's future ... *our* future. In *LAUNCH*, John Spencer and A.J. Juliani provide a process that can be incorporated into every class at every grade level ... even if you don't consider yourself a "creative teacher." And if you dare to innovate and view creativity as an essential skill, you will empower your students to change the world—starting right now.

Kids Deserve It!

Pushing Boundaries and Challenging Conventional Thinking

By Todd Nesloney and Adam Welcome
(@TechNinjaTodd, @awelcome)

In *Kids Deserve It!*, Todd and Adam encourage you to think big and make learning fun and meaningful for students. Their high-tech, high-touch, and highly engaging practices will inspire you to take risks, shake up the status quo, and be a champion for your students. While you're at it, you just might rediscover why you became an educator in the first place.

Escaping the School Leader's Dunk Tank

How to Prevail When Others Want to See You Drown

By Rebecca Coda and Rick Jetter
(@RebeccaCoda, @RickJetter)

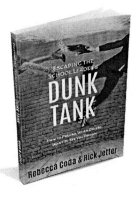

No school leader is immune to the effects of discrimination, bad politics, revenge, or ego-driven coworkers. These kinds of dunk-tank situations can make an educator's life miserable. By sharing real-life stories and insightful research, the authors (who are dunk-tank survivors themselves) equip school leaders with the practical knowledge and emotional tools necessary to survive and, better yet, avoid getting "dunked."

Your School Rocks…So Tell People!

Passionately Pitch and Promote the Positives Happening on Your Campus

By Ryan McLane and Eric Lowe
(@McLane_Ryan, @EricLowe21)

Great things are happening in your school every day. The problem is, no one beyond your school walls knows about them. School principals Ryan McLane and Eric Lowe want to help you get the word out! In *Your School Rocks … So Tell People!*, McLane and Lowe offer more than seventy immediately actionable tips along with easy-to-follow instructions and links to video tutorials. This practical guide will equip you to create an effective and manageable communication strategy using social media tools. Learn how to keep your students' families and community connected, informed, and excited about what's going on in your school.

Teaching Math with Google Apps

50 G Suite Activities

By Alice Keeler and Diana Herrington
(@AliceKeeler, @mathdiana)

Google Apps give teachers the opportunity to interact with students in a more meaningful way than ever before, while G Suite empowers students to be creative, critical thinkers who collaborate as they explore and learn. In *Teaching Math with Google Apps*, educators Alice Keeler and Diana Herrington demonstrate fifty different ways to bring math classes to the twenty-first century with easy-to-use technology.

Table Talk Math

*A Practical Guide for Bringing Math
into Everyday Conversations*

By John Stevens (@Jstevens009)

Making math part of families' everyday conversations is a powerful way to help children and teens learn to love math. In *Table Talk Math*, John Stevens offers parents (and teachers!) ideas for initiating authentic, math-based conversations that will get kids to notice and be curious about all the numbers, patterns, and equations in the world around them.

Shift This!

*How to Implement Gradual Changes for
MASSIVE Impact in Your Classroom*

By Joy Kirr

Establishing a student-led culture that isn't focused on grades and homework but on individual responsibility and personalized learning, may seem like a daunting task—especially if you think you have to do it all at once. But significant change is possible, sustainable, and even easy when it happens little by little. In *Shift This!* educator and speaker Joy Kirr explains how to make gradual shifts—in your thinking, teaching, and approach to classroom design—that will have a massive impact in your classroom. Make the first shift today!

About the Authors

Catherine "Missy" Lennard has over twenty years of experience as an educator and over fifteen years as an elementary school administrator. Missy has served as a principal for most of her career and still leads the school she opened in 2009. She has mentored many aspiring and early career administrators, and she is a lead principal in her district. She is passionate about empowering teachers and growing positive school cultures.

Julie Hasson was a school administrator for ten years before recently becoming a professor and coordinator of the Educational Leadership Program in the School of Education at Florida Southern College. When she is not writing, collaborating, and conspiring with her Purposeful Principals partner, Julie teaches and mentors graduate students and preservice teachers. Julie earned her doctorate at the University of South Florida in 2011.

Together, Missy and Julie formed Purposeful Principals in 2014 with a mission to help fellow educators teach and lead with more peace, hope, and purpose. Through writing, speaking, and coaching, they focus on changing limiting patterns into empowering practices in classrooms and schools across the nation.

Connect with Missy and Julie

 PURPOSEFULPRINCIPALS.COM

 @PPRINCIPALS #UNMAPPEDED

 FACEBOOK.COM/PURPOSEFULPRINCIPALS

CPSIA information can be obtained
at www.ICGtesting.com
Printed in the USA
FFOW01n2036090618
47077571-49493FF